The EU Fiscal Crisis: Forcing Eurozone Political Union in 2011?

By Graham Bishop

Searching finance

First published 2011 by Searching Finance Ltd, 8 Whitehall Road, London W7 2JE, UK

ISBN: 978-1-907720-14-7

Typeset by: Deirdré Gyenes

The EU Fiscal Crisis: Forcing Eurozone Political Union in 2011?

By Graham Bishop

Searching finance

About the author

Graham Bishop graduated from Sheffield University in 1972 with a degree in Jurisprudence. His publications, articles and speeches on the deregulation of Europe's financial markets provide an informed commentary from the practical perspective of a market participant, but with a political grounding.

His City career encompasses Phillips & Drew, S G Warburg, and Salomon Brothers/ Citigroup. He founded GrahamBishop.com in 2000 to bring directly to his clients the insights that flow from his standing as a leading technical analyst of economic and structural developments in the financial markets of Europe, providing an informed commentary from the practical perspective of a market participant, but with a political grounding. He has worked extensively with both European and UK political authorities, including the European Commission, where he was a member of the Consultative Group on the Impact of the Euro on Capital Markets (the Giovaninni Group). He was also a member of the Commission's Strategy Group on Financial Services (1998 – creating the Financial Services Action Plan) and the Committee of Independent Experts on the preparation of the changeover to the single currency (1994–95). He was nominated by the European Parliament to be one of its two members of the first Inter-Institutional Monitoring Group, and was Rapporteur for the spring 2003 and November 2004 Reports. He was elected to the Board of the Kangaroo Group in November, 2005 and re-elected in 2007 and 2009. In the UK's House of Commons, Mr Bishop was a Special Advisor to the Treasury Select Committee in its examination in 2003 of the implications for United Kingdom membership of the Single Currency. He advised the Treasury Committee on the corresponding reports in 1998 and 1996. He was also a Specialist Adviser to the House of Lords Select Committee on the European Union in its 2003 inquiry into *The Barriers to Competition in the Internal Market for Financial Services*. He is a Council Member of the Federal Trust and a member of the European League for Economic Co-operation (ELEC). He frequently participates in studies and meetings of research institutes such as Centre for the Study of Financial Innovation (CSFI).

To keep up to date with Graham Bishop's comments, visit http://www.grahambishop.com/StaticJoinFreeNewsletter.aspx

About Searching Finance

Searching Finance Ltd is a dynamic new voice in knowledge provision for the financial services and related professional sectors. Our mission is to provide expert, highly relevant and actionable information and analysis, written by professionals, for professionals. For more information, please visit www.searchingfinance.com

Also available from Searching Finance

Effective Bank Regulation and Supervision: Lessons from the Financial Crisis – "Required reading for anyone with a stake in strengthening the financial system."
Robert P. Kelly, Chairman and CEO, BNY Mellon

The Outlook for European Payments 2011

Contents

Preface

In early 2011, the eurozone debt crisis looks likely to take a dramatic turn for the worse – raising the intensity of the search for enduring solutions as the markets now price six states as 'risky'.

In a little-noticed pre-Christmas statement, the eurozone leaders collectively affirmed "that they stand ready to do whatever is required to ensure the stability of the euro area as a whole. The euro is and will remain a central part of European integration." Chancellor Merkel of Germany and President Sarkozy of France also sent New Year messages to their citizens that cast the issue in terms that were both stark and historic.

Since the decisions at the fateful crisis weekend in mid-May 2010 which created a structure to resolve the situation in Greece, it has been increasingly clear that the eurozone was going to take tough collective action on the economic governance of its members. Its leaders have committed to enacting by June 2011 the European Commission's detailed proposals – even if the many critics regard them as still lacking in effective sanctions. But they do contain truly radical plans to intervene in the domestic economic affairs of members – if it becomes apparent that serious imbalances are brewing that could infect their fellow members via financial contagion.

It was also made dramatically clear to private lenders to 'imbalanced' states that they will face default risk in the future. This precipitated an immediate re-assessment of the creditworthiness of some states – exemplified by the run on Irish banks to the tune of about 100% of GDP once their guarantor was itself doubted. In parallel, the eurozone took upon itself, rather than the EU as a whole, the task of financing its members that were unable to access market financing – provided they agreed to 'strict conditionality'.

If the eurozone does indeed do "whatever is required", then it will survive. A political entity will emerge that will be characterised by a centralised funding of public debts that result from a collective oversight of many detailed aspects of economic life designed to improve competitiveness. "The policy prescriptions could potentially address fiscal, wage, macro-structural and macro-prudential policy aspects". Many observers will describe this as a loose federation called 'Eurozone'.

The leaders described the risks in their New Year messages in dramatic, even cataclysmic, terms. Failure of the euro is seen as unacceptable because it would lead to an unravelling of 'Europe'. Why do they say that?

A glance at the evolution of the European Union once it moved on from being a 'gleam in the eye' of far-sighted statesmen shows that the political goals were always to be reached "through concrete achievements which first create a de facto solidarity". Those practical achievements were the steps to create a single market giving "free movement of people, goods, services and capital". The single market is by no means complete but is universally seen as delivering enormous benefits to the citizens of Europe – not only in terms of growth and employment, but also the quality of life.

If things happened that smashed the concrete achievements, then it is a fair bet that the solidarity would vanish soon afterwards as the blame was spread around for the destruction of the benefits. The existence of the euro – together with a financial system that enables its daily use by 330 million people – is a major component of delivering the benefits of the single market as goods and services can now be purchased very easily across borders. But its existence also enables citizens to protect themselves very quickly against the risk of break-up by moving their money away from risk and towards safety.

So the eurozone – acting collectively – must move swiftly and decisively to convince lenders who have grown sceptical after a decade of failed promises from finance ministers. The lenders need to be sure that sound fiscal policies are put in place and will be adhered to – no matter what the short-term unpleasantness for citizens. It is now clear that without that reassurance, they will take their money elsewhere.

But there remains a scenario that has a good outcome. It requires a truly credible policy framework in combination with a collective financial facility that is manifestly big enough to fund all states at risk until the benefits of the new policies come through. That may require a quadrupling of the existing European Financial Stability Fund (EFSF) facility so that it has the capacity to disburse €1 trillion of loans that will be repaid if the recipients perform as they have promised. The potential recipients have agreed already to the principles, and must swiftly turn them into detailed plans that they are seen to implement. Then the option for the core states of issuing guarantees they have good reason to expect not to be called will seem much better than facing actual cash losses from defaulted bank loans that are twice the guarantees.

Eurozone will have emerged from the financial crisis as a political federation – loose in some respects, but with tightly centralised economic governance at its heart. The proven commitment to fiscal probity may even make it attractive relative to alternative investments around the world.

Introduction

Winston Churchill – Zurich, 1946

"I am now going to say something that will astonish you. The first step in the re-creation of the European family must be a partnership between France and Germany. In this way only can France recover the moral and cultural leadership of Europe. There can be no revival of Europe without a spiritually great France and a spiritually great Germany. The structure of the United States of Europe will be such as to make the material strength of a single State less important. Small nations will count as much as large ones and gain their honour by a contribution to the common cause."

Schuman Declaration of 9 May, 1950

"Europe will not be made all at once, or according to a single plan. It will be built through concrete achievements which first create a de facto solidarity. The coming together of the nations of Europe requires the elimination of the age-old opposition of France and Germany. Any action taken must in the first place concern these two countries."

Sixty years after Robert Schuman's declaration – almost to the day – Europe faced its greatest political test and its leaders decided to support one of its members financially on a massive scale. 2011 seems likely to pose even tougher tests and the results could mark a turning point in the political evolution of Europe. The eurozone may cement a more collective form of economic governance, while other countries such as the UK, move further into the margins.

Consider the New Year messages from three political leaders:

- President Sarkozy of France: "Do not believe, my dear compatriots, those who propose that we leave the euro. The isolation of France would be folly. The end of the euro would be the end of Europe. I will oppose with all my might any step back that ignores 60 years of European construction, which brought peace and brotherhood in our continent… Europe is essential to our future, our identity and our values."
- Chancellor Merkel of Germany: "Europe has faced a big test in recent months. We have to strengthen the euro. It is not just about our money. The euro is much more than a currency. Fortunately, we Europeans are unified. A united Europe is the guarantor for our peace and freedom. The euro forms the basis of our prosperity. Germany needs Europe and our common currency, for our own well-being and also in order to overcome big challenges worldwide."
- Prime Minister Cameron: His message did not mention the word 'Europe'.

The comments from the eurozone contain two elements: preserving the economic gains from European integration – maintaining the single market – and an external dimension of Europe's place on the world stage. In the financial sphere, the EU is already projecting its power via soft economic influence that comes from trade. But it also stems from exporting its legislative model around the world to any country that wants to modernise its financial legislation with single, modern measures such as IFRS, UCITS, MiFID, Solvency II, and the EU's influence on the G20 process, Basel etc.

However, the EU will soon have to reshape some of its financial regulations to reflect the imminent victory in the real world of the 'bond market vigilantes' over the macro-econometricians who have ballooned public debts until their sustainability has been challenged. That may produce profound political change, even during 2011: a volcanic eruption is developing from which a loose political federation called 'Eurozone' may well crystallise.

Overview

The EU Fiscal Crisis: Forcing Eurozone Political Union in 2011?

This book examines the responses to the economic and fiscal crisis and the direction being taken towards European political integration. It looks at the development of the single market in 2010, regulatory issues in the EU and wider economic pressures. It analyses how and why the implications are for integration rather than disintegration. At the end of the crisis, Eurozone will have emerged as a political federation – loose in some respects, but with tightly centralised economic governance at its heart. The proven commitment to fiscal probity may even make it attractive relative to alternative investments around the world.

Part I covers the development of the single market in financial services in 2010 and the plans for 2011. It gives some specific examples of the continuing process of deepening the single market. There seems to be no visible intention to back-track on this – at least in the financial sphere. Indeed, the logic of the G20 process is to force more policy co-ordination at the global level and the simplest way for the European Union to deliver on these commitments to its global trading partners is to press forward with an even deeper single market.

So the wave of EU-level regulatory activity is set to grow. These actions are Schuman's "concrete achievements" and they have certainly created a "de facto solidarity". Would they, or even could they, endure a massive shock to that solidarity in the form of a disorderly and rancorous break-up of EMU? The EU has already decided to drive this deepening forward just at a moment when the political strains from the financial crisis seem set to sharpen.

Topics covered in Part I include:

- The critical importance that, in the forthcoming legislative decisions to be made by Parliament and Council, the implications on the single market for financial services be given central consideration. The supervisory structures that have just come to life are likely to mark the EU's financial landscape for a long time.

  It would be a serious strategic mistake if the Council, under the pressure of Member States giving priority to a natural tendency to protect national supervisory competences, were to favour timid solutions. These would create the risk of a fragmented and more vulnerable single market.
- Any citizen who fears that his home state is about to leave the euro to implement a major devaluation can transfer their liquid funds into a bank in another eurozone state – in an instant and at negligible cost. In effect, this is a free option for all citizens and amounts to an instantaneous referendum on government policy. Such an outflow of retail liquidity from a banking system would cause its rapid collapse as even the new Basel III proposals on liquidity assume retail deposits to be particularly stable. The quiet run out of deposits in the Irish banks last year demonstrated the power of depositors to force radical political change.
- The perennial problem of 'more Europe or less Europe'. It may well be that the only way to achieve the objective of providing a high level of consumer protection with that of creating a genuine single market is 'full harmonisation' of some specific, targeted measures.

- 2011 will see a raft of detailed proposals that will pave the way to consumers becoming more accustomed to a genuinely single market in financial services. As time goes by, citizens will find that their everyday life is increasingly bound up with cross-border financial activity and the loss of the single currency would cause a major disruption to their life.
- A single set of accounting standards is an absolute necessity. Owners of a security must know what assets and income are backing it. So they must understand completely the accounting standards that define these financial variables.

  The power of the EU to create global influence for such standards may well be matched with equally dramatic internal implications during the next decade. In the current fiscal crisis, tax revenues are a vital resource for any state and a single set of accounting standards may promote tax harmonisation.
- The role of the EU in the G20 and reform of financial regulations: Implementing global agreements – in the EU context – will inevitably mean another step forward in the intensity of the single market through the creation of resolution regimes (i.e. dismembering large bankrupt banks without destroying the economy).

Part II covers integrating European economic governance, with crisis as the driver in 2010 providing a stronger structure in 2011. It provides context to the current crisis, in terms of the political and legislative responses, examining the timetable of recent events in the eurozone and their implications.

The chances of future fiscal crises should not be understated. The integration of a single financial market emerges as a critical factor: should the EU move towards 'more Europe or less' in this field? Former Commissioner Mario Monti has pointed out that the EU is already committed to far-reaching reform as part of the G20 process and "It would be a serious strategic mistake ... to favour timid solutions."

At the very least, the Eurogroup must act together to change EU regulations to take proper account of the new reality they are imposing.

Topics covered in Part II include:

- When financial commentators talk glibly about the possible disintegration of the euro, they may not be thinking deeply about the full implications if such a process were accompanied by a fracturing of the carefully nurtured relationship between France and Germany. There is an alternative outcome to a fracturing: could the crisis instead lead to a deepening of the relationship that would run well beyond France and Germany and include all members of the eurozone?

  The Heads of Government announced "that they stand ready to do whatever is required to ensure the stability of the euro area as a whole. The euro is and will remain a central part of European integration."

  There is much media discussion about the opposite result – some countries leaving the euro. Anxious depositors would have plenty of time to remove their deposits from banks in any states that might leave. The natural and logical consequence of a collapse of all banks in those states may deter politicians from going down that route.
- The crisis as a eurozone issue: The driving force is the belated recognition by eurozone political leaders that the nature of their debts was fundamentally altered when they gave up the power to print money to repay such debts. Given the huge scale of public debts, markets are now posing an even more fundamental question: will political leaders countenance an even higher degree of solidarity

than they agreed as recently as May? The solution to these questions is increasingly a eurozone rather than EU issue – a bifurcation that may well prove to be a turning point of historic significance.

So the eurozone, rather than the whole EU, should be responsible for dealing with all future ramifications of this crisis.

- The chances of a Treaty change being agreed and ratified within the timescale of a rapidly rising fiscal crisis are close to nil. Practical solutions to this crisis must be found within existing institutional arrangements. In the decades ahead, the eurozone may prove that its collective economic governance arrangements really do force its members to pursue fiscally sound policies, so adopting joint liabilities could well be non-controversial at that distant stage.

Finally, Part III examines the vital issue of how financial integration will force political integration of the eurozone in 2011 and later. It looks at the immediate state of government bond issuance, economic governance, the role of sanctions and of financial assistance.

Topics covered in Part III include:

- Policymakers must move back to first principles swiftly to ensure that no Member State can ever blackmail the Union again. The approach must be as rigorous and comprehensive as the reforming response to the private sector crisis because the Union has been proven beyond all reasonable doubt to have defective disciplining mechanisms. This is the challenge for 2011.
- The backdrop to a series of potentially difficult bond issues by risky states will be a string of rows among EU policymakers that may make market participants wonder how serious the Member States really are about preventing any

recurrence of this type of fiscal crisis. The Commission's autumn forecasts still point to rising debt burdens this year and next in the risky states – in some case quite sharply.

- The eurozone now faces several options for its future actions. Considering specific scenarios may be the best mechanism to illustrate the choices that must be made and each scenario simply lays out the developments that flow logically after each choice. Three scenarios are considered: an inflationary debt spiral; default; or the emergence of a collectively strong, federal eurozone.
- Once the Head of Government of the core states realise that their banks have lent 23% of their assets (€1.9 trillion) to the six states now deemed risky by the markets, they have little choice but to continue swiftly to cement rigorous fiscal consolidation and enhanced competitiveness. With that assured, the EFSF should be roughly quadrupled so that €1 trillion is capable of being disbursed to fund the risky states for say the next three years until the benefits of the restructuring are clear.
- A political federation called Eurozone with 330 million people will have emerged.

Part I
The development of the single market in financial services in 2010 and the direction for 2011

Searching finance

Introduction

Schuman's call for "concrete achievements" was delivered decisively in 1985 by an agreement to amend the Treaty of Rome with a Single European Act. This gave the famous 'four freedoms': free movement of goods, services, people and capital. As Margaret Thatcher put it afterwards, "What we need are strengths which we can only find together... We must have the full benefit of a single large market." Ever since, the imperative has been to make such lofty goals operational in practice.

That imperative continues powerfully and the Competitiveness Council noted in December 2010 "that the single market is one of the greatest achievements of the EU. It has indeed helped to increase growth by 1.85% and to create 2.75 million additional jobs in the period 1992–2009 and ... that the single market remains the cornerstone of the EU project which needs to be continuously adapted and much more developed in order to realise similarly big gains in the future. Indeed the single market remains fragmented in various areas, which constitutes a strong constraint for enterprises, in particular for small and medium-sized enterprises (SMEs), and also for citizens; considers that all these elements make crucial an ambitious relaunch of the single market and stresses the need for a well functioning single market..."

In part, the governments of the EU were responding collectively to the European Commission's Work Programme for 2011 – announced in October. These proposals all represent a 'single market' approach to the problems that had surfaced so devastatingly in the EU's financial system. If there are to be cross-border financial institutions to deliver the efficiency gains of the single market, then correspondingly there must be 'more Europe' to enforce appropriate regulation. In the last resort, there must even be European-level powers to restructure failed banks.

Financial regulation: completing the reform

A comprehensive timeline for delivery of proposals to complete the EU's financial reform was presented in June 2010. Early in 2011, the Commission will table the remaining proposals to complete the financial sector reform.

Most of the proposals to address the flaws exposed by the crisis are already agreed or on the table, with the recent agreements on the financial supervision package as a milestone. In the first half of 2011, the Commission will follow up with a further series of improvements to bank capital rules (CRD IV) to implement within the EU the outcome of international work in the Basel Committee on Banking Standards, changes to the Market in Financial Instruments Directive (MiFID) and the Market Abuse Directive to complete the move to more transparent and safer derivates markets, a proposal on Credit Rating Agencies, as well as legislation establishing a framework for bank crisis management and resolution to equip the relevant authorities with a consistent set of tools including resolution funds.

A particular focus will be the protection of small investors and ordinary consumers: initiatives will include legislation on access to basic banking services, and action to promote responsible lending and borrowing practice on mortgages.

These and other proposals will complete the Commission's ambitious reform programme for the financial sector. A joint goal of the European institutions should be to have the full reform agreed by the end of 2011, thus putting in place an advanced system of financial regulation as one of the foundation stones for healthy, job-creating growth. Meanwhile, the EU will continue its efforts to promote a strong and co-ordinated global approach, notably through its active participation in the G20.

Source: Commission Work Programme 2011, section 2.2

That work programme reflected the recommendations made by Professor Mario Monti and delivered to Commission President Barroso in May 2010. By coincidence, this was in the week after the historic crisis meeting of the European Council that created a structure to resolve the immediate fiscal crisis in Greece. The Monti Report was a clarion call to ensure the single market in finance was not fractured. In October, Commissioner Michel Barnier went further and announced "today the Single Market Act sets out 50 proposals to be put into place by 2012 to make the Single Market work better." The symbolism is also powerful: an end-date 20 years after the original Single Market programme was delivered.

The single market for capital and financial services

Supervision for a single market, not fragmentation of the market through supervision

The single market for capital and the closely interrelated single market for financial services are critical for the efficient allocation of resources – a key driver of growth and employment – and for the stability of the economy. In the Seventies and Eighties, particularly in Europe, a tight system of restrictions to competition and constraints on allocation in the financial services industry, often designed to favour the financing of public sector deficits, had negative implications for investments and growth. The subsequent phase of financial liberalisation since the Nineties, not accompanied – particularly in the United States – by corresponding improvements in prudential regulation and supervision, was a key determinant of the financial crisis.

The European Union, also in the context of the G20, is currently engaged in an ambitious programme with the objective of putting in place an adequate supervisory system. The programme was triggered by the De Larosière Report, commissioned by the European Commission.

In this area, the policy process is being pursued as a matter of priority by the EU institutions. It does not appear necessary for the present report to review such ongoing work.

What does appear necessary, however, is to stress the critical importance that, in the forthcoming legislative decisions to be made by Parliament and Council, the implications on the single market for financial services be given central consideration. The supervisory structures that will be put in place following those decisions are likely to mark the EU's financial landscape for a long time.

It would be a serious strategic mistake if the Council, under the pressure of Member States giving priority to a natural tendency to protect national supervisory competences, were to favour timid solutions. These would present the risk of leading to a fragmented and more vulnerable single market.

Supporting the single market and financial integration, through the issuance of E-bonds

The EU needs a modern and developed financial system, built around a liquid risk-free asset class, which – being the benchmark for pricing other assets – would provide the basis for efficiently performing the essential functions of allocating resources, intermediating savings to investment, supporting better risk sharing and ensuring a more uniform transmission of the single monetary policy across the euro area. This would reinforce the strengths of the Single Market, underpin the euro as a global currency and support the smooth functioning of the EU economies, during normal times but also in the face of external shocks and financial crises, ultimately amplifying the growth and jobs dividend for Member States.

The government bond market has acted as a catalyst in fostering the integration of European financial markets since the creation of the euro, supported by the emergence of a larger and diversified investor base, reducing transaction and financing costs for governments, and in turn spurring the development of markets for other related asset classes (such as corporate bonds, covered bonds, asset-backed securities and a range of derivative instruments).

Source: Monti Report

So 2010 marked a series of reviews of the role of the Single Market during the period of extreme financial turbulence. At one level, it could have been argued that the Single Market in both money and financial services had *allowed* financial shocks to be transmitted from one country to another. However, the comparison with the economic shocks after say the Oil Crisis of 1974 showed clearly that shocks would be transmitted one way or another. Then, it was sharp currency devaluations and dramatic changes in interest rates as well as budgets. This time round, there was not even any discussion about the relative merits of maintaining the single market, and the collective decision of the Member States was to proceed rapidly in 2011 to deepen it, in many and detailed ways. This process will steadily cement the collective influence of Europe as a whole.

In this section, four particular examples of the continuing drive to complete the single market will be examined in some detail. They have been selected from many possible examples to illustrate the ever-increasing influence of the single market in welding Europe into a single economic unit:

- SEPA;
- Consumer protection;
- Accounting standards; and
- G20 process.

SEPA (Single Euro Payments Area)

This author has always argued strongly that there will not be a genuine single currency until citizens can make payments throughout the eurozone as easily, cheaply and safely as they can in their home country. If a payment costs €20–30 to make and is time-consumingly complex, then few individuals will bother with cross-border trade in goods and services. The Payments Services Directive was agreed in 2007 to resolve many of these issues. Whilst 'payments' are an intensely technical area, the political implications are immense – and completely underestimated by the political class.

In particular, this author participated in the design of the changeover to the euro in 1999 and the group was insistent on a complete change-over of notes and coins to create 'one money' because that made the monetary union process almost irreversible. With SEPA, any citizen who fears that his home state is about to leave the euro to implement a major devaluation can protect themselves by transferring their liquid funds into a bank in another eurozone state – in an instant and at negligible cost. In effect, this is a free option for all citizens and amounts to an instantaneous referendum on government policy. Such an outflow of retail liquidity from a banking system would cause its rapid collapse as even the new Basel III proposals on liquidity assume retail deposits to be particularly stable. The quiet run out of deposits in the Irish banks last year demonstrated the power of depositors to force radical political change.

Many elements of the SEPA scheme went live in 2009 but the ECB Director Gertrude Tumpel-Gugerell pointed out that SEPA is built on a further column: SEPA for cards. Cards are the most commonly used payment instrument in the European Union, accounting for almost four out of ten transactions in 2008. Without the success of SEPA for cards, the project will not be complete. But SEPA for cards is about much more than that: it is about business rules and technical standards.

The SEPA Council met for the first time in June 2010 and brought together top-level representatives from both the demand and supply sides of the European payments market, under the co-chairmanship of the European Commission and the European Central Bank (ECB), the two institutions that have led the creation of this new body. The main issues discussed were the need and conditions to establish migration end-date(s) for SEPA, and the future of a SEPA for payment cards.

According to a European Commission survey, 32 European countries now participate in SEPA, more than 4,400 banks have joined the SEPA credit transfer scheme, and more than 3,000 banks have signed up for the SEPA direct debit scheme. Hence, much has been achieved in implementing SEPA. However, further action by European legislators is needed for SEPA to be completed successfully. A mandatory timeline for the migration to SEPA payment instruments will significantly accelerate the pace of transition, enabling SEPA to be completed, preferably, by the end of 2012 for credit transfers, and by the end of 2013 for direct debits.

Other key elements for the success of SEPA that still need to be addressed include: the provision of innovative payment services (e.g. online and mobile payment services), the creation of an additional European card scheme, and the enhancement of the security of card transactions by phasing out the magnetic stripe on European cards. European Payments Council (EPC) Chair Gerard Hartsink has stressed that it is now up to EU lawmakers to provide planning security to all market participants by setting a clear deadline for migration to the SEPA schemes. The Eurosystem announced its preferred SEPA migration end-dates of 2012 for credit transfers and the end of 2013 for direct debits.

In December, Commissioner Michel Barnier responded with a formal proposal and said: "We have a single market, many countries share a single currency and soon we will move to a single pan-European payments system in Europe. It means that making payments cross-border will become as easy as making them at home. Consumers will only need one bank account and their payments will be faster, cheaper and safer. Businesses will benefit from one set of standards and much simpler processes. The proposal adopted today fixes end-dates to make this pan-European system a reality, hopefully as early as 2012." The Commission's proposal now passes to the European Parliament and the Member States for consideration.

During 2011, another legislative step will be taken to make the single currency ever more irreversible.

Consumer protection

The goal of a single financial market for consumers was one of the driving forces for the creation of a single currency. However, the financial crisis showed rather dramatically that there were risks lurking for the unwary consumer – most vividly for foreign customers of Icelandic banks and Northern Rock, though non-UK customers of Equitable Life were also left exposed a decade ago. Investors who found they had been sucked into the Madoff fraud also wonder how they could have been left unprotected.

So the Commission launched a consultation in July 2010 into virtually every aspect of consumer protection – both domestic and cross-border. As Commissioner Barnier said, "European consumers deserve better. They need reassurance that their savings, investments or insurance policies are protected no matter where in Europe they are based." There were some concrete proposals as well as consultation:

- Bank accounts: for bank account holders, the measures adopted mean that in case their bank failed, they would receive their money back faster (within seven days), increased coverage (up to €100,000) and better information on how and when they are protected.
- Insurance: options to improve protection for insurance policy holders, including the possibility of setting up Insurance Guarantee Schemes in all Member States.
- Investors: for investors who use investment services, the Commission proposed faster compensation if an investment firm fails to return the investor's assets due to fraud, administrative malpractice or operational errors, while the level of compensation is to go up from €20,000 to €50,000. Investors will also receive better information on when the compensation scheme would apply and get better protection against fraudulent misappropriations where their assets are held by a third party – such as in the recent Madoff affair.

This latest consultation is but one in a long line of reviews, and some action. Whilst the driving force may be the desire to create a pan-EU retail financial market, there are still many problems within national markets. Last year, then-Consumer Commissioner Meglena Kuneva argued that "Retail bankers are letting consumers down. There is widespread evidence that basic consumer principles are being violated with problems from complex pricing to hidden charges and information that is unclear and incomplete. Banks need to put their house in order with a culture change in the way they treat customers. And Member State Authorities need to fulfil their obligation to enforce EU consumer laws." The latter comment was focused on some aspects of the 2008 Consumer Credit Directive.

However, these goals bring into focus the perennial problem of 'more Europe or less Europe'. It may well be that the only way to achieve the objective of providing a high level of consumer protection with that of creating a genuine single market is 'full harmonisation' of some specific, targeted measures.

In 2009, there was a public consultation on the Green Paper on the Retail Financial Services as 'tying' was identified by financial services users as a key barrier to the integration of EU retail financial services markets. Another report on bank charges cited specific problems including information which is often difficult to understand, opaque bank fees, problems with advice and low levels of switching. That report described the price structures of current accounts as "very opaque, making it almost impossible for consumers to know how much they are paying and to compare different offers." After the financial crisis, 'responsible lending' is the watchword so credit products should be appropriate for consumers' needs and be tailored to their ability to repay. Correspondingly, 'responsible borrowing' is expected so consumers should provide relevant, complete and accurate information.

There is a now single currency and consumers are able to make cross-border payments easily. All participants in retail financial markets should expect further rounds of legislation to ensure that consumers are adequately protected – both in their home market and cross-border. 2011 will see a raft of detailed proposals that will pave the way to consumers becoming more accustomed to a genuinely single market in financial services. As time goes by, citizens will find that their everyday life is increasingly bound up with cross-border financial activity and the loss of the single currency would cause a major disruption to their life.

Accounting standards

As the EU began to tackle the issues that had to be resolved in order to create a single market in capital, it was immediately obvious that a single set of accounting standards was an absolute necessity. Owners of a security must know what assets and income are backing it. So they must understand completely the accounting standards that define these financial variables. Whatever may be said about visions of a pan-EU market, there was never a chance that a single set of existing national standards would be adopted by all the other Member States. However, the accounting bodies of several of the leading EU states had been involved with the International Accounting Standards Committee (IASC) since its foundation in 1983. As its objective was the creation of a single set of high-quality accounting standards, it was an easy decision to adopt International Accounting Standards (IAS) – as a matter of principle. This was done by an EU regulation in 2002 for the 7,000 listed companies – but each IAS was to be subject to a formal EU decision to give legal endorsement for use within the EU. That judgment implicitly carried the risk that the EU version of IAS might deviate from the texts agreed by the International Accounting Standards Board (IASB) itself.

The G20 agreed in 2008 that a major goal of global financial reform would be the use of a single set of high quality accounting standards and set the goal of convergence between US GAAP and IAS. The stage was set for something of a political power struggle between the US and the approximately 110 countries that had followed the EU's lead and adopted International Financial Reporting Standards (IFRS), or were in the process of doing so. In February 2010, the Financial Times reported that the IASB was no longer willing to pursue convergence with its US peer as "an objective in itself" – the latest sign of eroding consensus on accounting rules.

However, Gerrit Zalm (IASC Chairman) immediately wrote to the FT "I was surprised to read your interpretation of recent enhancements to the governance of the IASC Foundation ('IASB softens stance on convergence'), and in particular your assertion that a constitutional emphasis on adoption of IFRS represents a weakening of the Trustees' support for the ongoing work to converge global accounting standards... Nothing could be further from the truth..."

The issue of accounting standards for financial instruments had emerged in 2010 as a potentially major stumbling block to the whole convergence process. Amongst several major problems, the type of business model used by a bank was critical. The European perception was that the US wanted to 'fair value' all financial instruments held on the balance sheet. But EU banks argued that would introduce an unrealistic volatility to profits and that they should be allowed to account on the basis of loans that were unimpaired – if their business model was simply making loans and collecting the interest.

For example, the European Banking Federation pointed out "that the initial expected cash flow estimate is recognised over the life of the related assets, whereas the present value of (positive and negative) changes in the expected cash flow estimate must be recognised immediately. This results in significant additional subjectivity, volatility and pro-cyclicality." The reason for the intense focus on such technical minutiae was the impending revision of the capital adequacy standards for banks – Basel III. The rules defining the value of a bank's assets would flow straight through to the amount of capital it needed. Even worse, if the bank's international competitors were not subject to the same rules, then the competitive playing field would become decidedly un-level.

So some of the most detailed possible rules had turned into a major test for international co-operation – the G20 process itself was on trial. At the beginning of November 2010, the US Securities and Exchange Commission "directed the staff of the Office of the Chief Accountant of the SEC to develop and execute a work plan for the consideration of IFRS *as issued by the*

IASB [author's emphasis] into the US financial reporting system." The Staff had published the Work Plan in February 2010 and it included the following:

1 Sufficient development and application of IFRS for the US domestic reporting system; and
2 The independence of standard setting for the benefit of investors.

These two areas consider the characteristics of IFRS and its standard-setting process that would be the most relevant to a future determination by the Commission regarding whether to incorporate IFRS into the financial reporting system for US issuers. Since February 2010, the Staff has invested significant time and effort in executing the Work Plan. Many of the Staff's efforts are currently in process and are not expected to be completed until 2011, particularly as they relate to consideration of the two points listed above.

At the end of November 2010, the IASB updated its own work plan to reflect the changes according to the updated Convergence Report and to provide more detail on the expected timing of pronouncements. In the first quarter of 2011, they plan pronouncements on financial instruments – impairment and asset/liability offsetting (exposure drafts); and in the second quarter on financial instruments – impairment, hedge accounting, asset/liability offsetting. So the moment of decision will come at the end of the second quarter this year.

In a fascinating intervention in this debate in a speech at the FEI Conference in November, Harvey Goldschmid (a former SEC Commissioner who had been very influential) pointed out that IFRS were now at a critical crossroad: during the past decade – in a remarkable success story – IFRS have been accepted in more than 100 countries and are now actively under consideration in a dozen more (e.g. China, India and Japan). The goal of a single set of high-quality global accounting standards has been endorsed by the US government and the G20. "However, the next 14 months will be critical in determining whether the goal of a 'single set of high quality global standards' will be realised in the lifetimes of most of us. The SEC is committed to making an adoption decision in 2011 and this is the key to the future. I very much hope the Commission will act affirmatively. A negative decision on IFRS in 2011 by the SEC – or, as bad, a decision to delay an adoption commitment – would likely have tragic consequences. In such circumstances, two basic scenarios are probable:

"First, the coalition of nations supporting IFRS could break apart. Rather than two sets of accounting standards, IFRS and US GAAP, we could go back to pre-2000 fragmentation.

"The second basic scenario is even worse from a US perspective. The coalition in support of IFRS could hold and the US would become isolated. The US would no longer play the large and constructive role it now plays in IFRS development and oversight. I believe that without active US participation the overall quality of the international accounting standards would deteriorate. Remember, there is less concern about transparency and investor protection in some other parts of the world. I also believe that the US could not remain out of a global system forever."

In 2002, the European Union selected IFRS as its internal accounting standards and that seal of approval created the critical mass to propel them to become virtually *the* global standard. Within a decade, the economic superpower – the US – may find that it has little option but to go along with 'high-quality' global rules – *providing* they are demonstrably high quality. That would be a dramatic illustration of the growth of the European Union's soft economic power within the global economy.

The power of the EU to set such standards may well have equally dramatic internal implications during the next decade. In the current fiscal crisis, tax revenues are a vital resource for any state.

Tax issues have to be decided by unanimity of the EU Member States, so integration in that field has lagged. But a hot issue now is the application of suitable IFRS to small and medium-sized enterprises (SMEs). Once all corporations in the EU are subject to similar accounting standards to define their profits, it must be only a matter of time before 'tax competition' pushes individual Member States to take their own sovereign decisions to align their tax codes with accounting standards for the purpose of calculating taxable profits. At that stage, the competition for locating job-creating industry will only reflect the tax *rate*, rather than the tax *base*. As Ireland has just shown, that competition will be sharp indeed and the EU will have become an 'ever-closer union' even in vital tax matters – driven by the desire to have a single market.

The G20 and reform of financial regulations: the role of the EU

Declaration of the Summit on Financial Markets and the World Economy

We, the Leaders of the Group of Twenty[1], held an initial meeting in Washington on November 15, 2008, amid serious challenges to the world economy and financial markets. We are determined to enhance our co-operation and work together to restore global growth and achieve needed reforms in the world's financial systems.

[1] The members of the G20 are: Argentina, Australia, Brazil, Canada, China, European Union, France, Germany, India, Indonesia, Italy, Japan, Mexico, Russia, Saudi Arabia, South Africa, South Korea, Turkey, United Kingdom, United States

Common Principles for Reform of Financial Markets

8. In addition to the actions taken above, we will implement reforms that will strengthen financial markets and regulatory regimes so as to avoid future crises. Regulation is first and foremost the responsibility of national regulators who constitute the first line of defence against market instability. However, our financial markets are global in scope, therefore, intensified international co-operation among regulators and strengthening of international standards, where necessary, and their consistent implementation is necessary to protect against adverse cross-border, regional and global developments affecting international financial stability...

Reinforcing International Co-operation: We call upon our national and regional regulators to formulate their regulations and other measures in a consistent manner. Regulators should enhance their co-ordination and co-operation across all segments of financial markets, including with respect to cross-border capital flows. Regulators and other relevant authorities as a matter of priority should strengthen co-operation on crisis prevention, management, and resolution.

The Washington Summit in November 2008 changed the rules of financial regulation in many ways but for the purposes of this book, the key was setting international co-operation at the heart of policy-making. At times, that may look more of an aspiration than a binding agreement but many complex decisions have been taken already, and these have flowed downwards to legislative actions by the EU and thus into binding law at national level in EU Member States.

Much more will flow in the years ahead and a key element is that the EU – as five of the 20 members – consciously co-ordinates its position ahead of meetings so that its global influence is substantially reinforced by the G20 process. Thus a major Member State deciding to leave the EU would not escape from the reach of EU rules because they are merely implementing global decisions. If a state decided not to abide by such global decisions, it would risk becoming a global and not just a European pariah.

In April 2010, the G20 Finance Ministers and Central Bank Governors recommitted to developing by end-2010 internationally agreed rules to improve both the quantity and quality of bank capital and to discourage excessive leverage. The new rules would be phased in by end-2012 and be complemented by strong supervision. They also reiterated the importance of achieving a single set of high quality, global accounting standards and welcomed the work undertaken by the Financial Stability Board (FSB) on standards for central clearing and trading on exchanges for standardised over-the-counter (OTC) derivative contracts and their reporting to trade repositories.

Afterwards, FSB chairman Mario Draghi set out the timetable of reform proposals. The key priority is the revamp of the Basel capital framework and the liquidity standard, and he called for transition and grandfathering arrangements to avoid adverse macroeconomic impacts. On 'too big to fail' (TBTF), the two essential complements are the national resolution frameworks and improvements to financial infrastructure that reduce contagion risks, notably in the OTC derivatives market. The FSB presented a shortlist of likely policy options to the G20 Summit in June and a final package of recommendations to the November Summit. The FSB also established a working group, to report by October with policy options to increase the standardisation of OTC derivatives and to develop a clear process to implement consistently mandatory clearing and exchange or electronic trading requirements at the global level.

The EU continued to co-ordinate its position and Commission President Barroso wrote to EU President Van Rompuy and all members of the European Council, and to European Parliament

President Buzek, in view of the upcoming G20 Summit in Toronto on 26–27 June. In his letter President Barroso presented five key G20 deliverables, which he believes should be at the heart of a strong EU position for the Summit.

These included "Timely and consistent implementation of the existing commitments to reform financial markets, inter alia on rules to improve bank capital, implementation of the Financial Stability Board remuneration principles and accounting standards convergence. This should include agreement on a financial institution levy to reduce systemic risk and contribute to bank repair. Within the EU, the Commission is ready to deliver all remaining reform proposals in a way that would allow the European Council to set a political target for adoption of the reform already by the end of 2012, and we should press our partners to reciprocate."

President Barroso also pointed out that "The events of the past weeks have again exposed just how interconnected markets and economies around the world have become. The G20 remains a key vehicle for the EU to drive forward a reform agenda which tackles the challenges exposed and which commits our international partners to deliver too... The EU played a key role in launching the G20 leaders' process, and has provided much of the political impetus and substantive thinking that has established it as the primary forum for global discussion and co-ordination on economic and financial issues. The European Council on 17 June is set to finalise EU preparations of the G20 summit."

At the Toronto Summit shortly afterwards, G20 members did agree on a four-pillar reform agenda including financial infrastructures, capital standards, supervisory issues and resolution systems. However, the G20 member states also noted that the standards would be "phased in over a time frame that is consistent with sustained recovery and limits market disruption." Already they were becoming concerned in public about the risk of pushing the financial system too quickly to reach standards of prudence that might undermine an over-leveraged economy.

Ahead of the November G20 Summit in Seoul, Barroso and van Rompuy sent a joint letter to EU Heads of State which included some key messages:

- The G20 Summit in Seoul will be a real test of whether the G20 can continue to deliver in its role as the premier global forum for international economic co-operation.
- We need a clear common EU position on a set of difficult issues.
- G20 Framework for Strong, Balanced and Sustainable Growth: all G20 countries must recognise that economic imbalances are a common concern, and that all major economies must do their part to achieve rebalancing. If the debate on setting current accounts target came back at the table, we should underline the benefits of our own mechanism based on a limited number of indicators. In addition, we cannot ignore the recent exchange rate issues and should promote our shared interest in a strong and stable international financial system. The G20 should reaffirm its commitment to move towards more market-oriented exchange rate systems that reflect underlying economic fundamentals and refrain from competitive devaluation of currencies.
- Financial regulatory reform: the implementation and monitoring of key reforms like the Basel III agreement needs to be ensured. The agenda for financial regulatory reform has not yet been completed. Moreover, the EU should continue to support work in the G20 to explore and develop a financial transaction tax at global level. In the meantime, we need to work on other ways of ensuring that the financial sector makes an equitable contribution,

through measures such as a financial activities tax and levies.

At the G20 Seoul summit, leaders agreed that the transformation of the financial system to address the root causes of the crisis was essential and welcomed achievements from the mandate. The detail of these agreements underlined that there will be a further wave of reform of the financial system that will go to the heart of major cross-border financial institutions.

Implementing these global agreements – in the EU context – will inevitably mean another step forward in the intensity of the single market through the creation of resolution regimes (translation: dismembering large bankrupt banks without destroying the economy). The most difficult cases will be the globally 'systemically important financial institutions' (G-SIFI). The list has not yet been defined but EU members are likely to be 'home' for many of them and all will almost certainly have major activities in the EU. The UK is likely to be home to at least three – Barclays, HSBC and RBS – and each of them has a balance sheet larger than the UK's annual GDP.

Financial sector reforms

The global financial system came to a sudden halt in 2008 as a result of reckless and irresponsible risk-taking by banks and other financial institutions, combined with major failures of regulation and supervision. While our initial priority was to move quickly to stabilise financial markets and restore the global flow of capital, we never lost sight of the need to address the root causes of the crisis. We took our first step at the Washington Summit, where we developed the Action Plan to Implement Principles for Reform. Since then, we built on the progress made in London, Pittsburgh, and Toronto, and together, took major strides toward fixing the financial system with the support from the international organisations, particularly the Financial Stability Board (FSB) and the Basel Committee on Banking Supervision (BCBS).

Transformed financial system to address the root causes of the crisis

Today, we have delivered core elements of the new financial regulatory framework to transform the global financial system.

We endorsed the landmark agreement reached by the BCBS on the new bank capital and liquidity framework, which increases the resilience of the global banking system by raising the quality, quantity and international consistency of bank capital and liquidity, constrains the build-up of leverage and maturity mismatches, and introduces capital buffers above the minimum requirements that can be drawn upon in bad times. The framework includes an internationally harmonised leverage ratio to serve as a backstop to the risk-based capital measures. With this, we have achieved far-reaching reform of the global banking system. The new standards will markedly reduce banks' incentive to take excessive risks, lower the likelihood and severity of future crises, and enable banks to withstand – without extraordinary government support – stresses of a magnitude associated with the recent financial crisis. This will result in a banking system that can better support stable economic growth. We are committed to adopt and implement fully these standards within the agreed timeframe that is consistent with economic recovery and financial stability. The new framework will be translated into our national laws and regulations, and will be implemented starting on January 1, 2013 and fully phased in by January 1, 2019.

We reaffirmed our view that no firm should be too big or too complicated to fail and that taxpayers should not bear the costs of resolution. We endorsed the policy framework, work processes, and timelines proposed by the FSB to reduce the moral hazard risks posed by systemically important financial institutions (SIFIs) and address the too-big-to-fail problem. This requires a multi-pronged framework combining: a resolution framework and other measures to ensure that all financial institutions can be resolved safely, quickly and without destabilising the financial system and exposing the taxpayers to the risk of loss; a requirement that SIFIs and initially in particular financial institutions that are globally systemic (G-SIFIs) should have higher loss absorbency capacity to reflect the greater risk that the failure of these firms poses to the global financial system; more intensive supervisory oversight; robust core financial market infrastructure to reduce contagion risk from individual failures; and other supplementary prudential and other requirements as determined by the national authorities which may include, in some circumstances, liquidity surcharges, tighter large exposure restrictions, levies and structural measures. In the context of loss absorbency, we encourage further progress on the feasibility of contingent capital and other instruments. We encouraged the FSB, BCBS and other relevant bodies to complete their remaining work in accordance with the endorsed work processes and timelines in 2011 and 2012.

In addition, we agreed that G-SIFIs should be subject to a sustained process of mandatory international recovery and resolution planning. We agreed to conduct rigorous risk assessment on these firms through international supervisory colleges and negotiate institution-specific crisis cooperation agreements within crisis management groups.

Regular peer reviews will be conducted by the FSB on the effectiveness and consistency of national policy measures for these firms. We called on the FSB to build on this work and develop attributes of effective resolution regimes by 2011.

Delivering on our commitment in Toronto, we endorsed the policy recommendations prepared by the FSB in consultation with the IMF, on increasing supervisory intensity and effectiveness. We reaffirmed that the new financial regulatory framework must be complemented with more effective oversight and supervision. We agreed that supervisors should have strong and unambiguous mandates, sufficient independence to act, appropriate resources, and a full suite of tools and powers to proactively identify and address risks, including regular stress testing and early intervention.

Source: G20 Seoul Summit Document, November 2010

Conclusions on the impact of the single market

The first part of this book has given some specific examples of the continuing process of deepening the single market. There seems to be no visible intention to back-track on this – at least in the financial sphere. Indeed, the logic of the G20 process is to force more policy co-ordination at the global level and the simplest way for the European Union to deliver on these commitments to its global trading partners is to press forward with an even deeper single market.

But that interlocks the citizens of EU Member States ever more closely in their financial transactions, and thus business. The examples already quoted are not intended to create an exhaustive list as it could easily be extended to include:

- The ripples from the crisis spread steadily wider and the auditors are now coming under scrutiny, quite apart from the standards that they apply. Commissioner Barnier wondered aloud why the audit firms did not see this crisis coming as they were in the front line of financial reporting.

So he launched a consultation on whether audits provide the right information to all financial participants or not. 70% of the European market is in the hands of the 'Big Four' and the crisis highlighted failings in the audit sector. "I believe it is important to approach this discussion in a frank and open manner. No subject should be taboo."

- The Commission outlined its vision for taxing the financial sector. At a global level, the Commission supports the idea of a Financial Transactions Tax (FTT) but at EU level, they recommend a Financial Activities Tax (FAT). This idea found favour with the Economic and Financial Affairs Council (ECOFIN) though there was recognition of the risk of competitive distortions and multiple charging of cross-border banks. In fact, Council called for consideration of the cumulative impact of all the measures on capital, liquidity, funding deposit guarantees etc.
- The FSB published a report on improving OTC derivatives markets with 21 recommendations on practical issues such as standardisation, central clearing, exchange or electronic platform trading, and reporting of OTC derivatives transactions. Coincidentally, the International Swaps and Derivatives Association (ISDA) Mid-Year 2010 Market Survey threw up some eye-catching numbers: the total notional amount outstanding of interest rate, credit, and equity derivatives was US$466.8 trillion (for reference: global GDP is around US$50 trillion) and the 14 largest international derivatives dealers account for 82% of that. Each of them has a net credit exposure, before collateral, averaging US$160 billion. As former Committee of European Securities Regulators (CESR) chairman Eddy Wymeersch put it at SIBOS "The real answer is that we have to look at reducing risks in these markets. You may

pile up all the collateral you want but in the event of crisis, collateral loses its value and solidarity disappears."

This is the backdrop to EMIR (European Market Infrastructure Regulation). The Commission proposed that standard OTC derivative contracts be cleared through central counterparties (CCPs). This will reduce counterparty credit risk, i.e. the risk that one party to the contract defaults. The Commission's proposal, fully in line with the EU's G20 commitments and the approach adopted by the United States, has now passed to the European Parliament and the EU Member States for consideration. Once adopted, the regulation would apply from end-2012.

Commissioner Barnier said: "No financial market can afford to remain a Wild West territory. OTC derivatives have a big impact on the real economy: from mortgages to food prices. The absence of any regulatory framework for OTC derivatives contributed to the financial crisis and the tremendous consequences we are all suffering from. Today, we are proposing rules which will bring more transparency and responsibility to derivatives markets. So we know who is doing what, and who owes what to whom. As well as taking action so that single failures do not destabilise the whole financial system, as was the case with Lehman's collapse."

So the wave of EU level regulatory activity is set to grow. These actions are Schuman's "concrete achievements" and they have certainly created a "de facto solidarity". Would they, or even could they, endure a massive shock to that solidarity in the form of a disorderly and rancorous break-up of EMU? The EU has already decided to drive this deepening forward just at a moment when the political strains from the financial crisis seem set to sharpen.

Part II

Integrating European economic governance: crisis as the driver in 2010 to providing a stronger structure in 2011

Searching finance

Background

Aggregate public debts in the EU rose from 32% of GDP in 1974 to 59% in 1989 as the Maastricht Treaty was being negotiated. They hit 70% in 1997 despite the new Treaty rules, but the reformed Stability and Growth Pact (SGP) succeeded in pushing the ratio just below 60% in 2008 – though largely driven by reduced interest expenditure. For the eurozone, the European Commission now expects (autumn 2010 Forecast) the debt ratio to hit 87% in 2011. By an unfortunate coincidence, the withdrawal of the fiscal stimulus seems likely to collide with the expected rise in age-related expenditures as the baby-boomers retire.

Realistically, it may be wishful thinking to expect the baby-boomers to vote for a major and sustained fiscal consolidation as they move into expensive old age. Without that, the Commission expects about half of eurozone members to see their public debt ratios exceed 100% of GDP in the next decade. So the chances of future fiscal crises may not be insignificant.

With the benefit of hindsight, the temptation by civic society to keep voting for an easy way out of fiscal problems has always been a likely outcome. Greece has demonstrated the point convincingly, and sections of UK society still seem to hanker after this approach despite the commitments made by the Coalition parties elected in May 2010. But these are not isolated examples after the baby-boomer generation discovered that public debt could be used to offset unpleasant external events after the first Oil Shock of 1973–75. The subsequent trend in public debt is disturbing, underlining the broad discussion about its sustainability.

The political response to the current crisis

Two decades ago, no one remotely foresaw the expansion and thus ultimate scale of the globalised financial system. Accordingly, no thought was given to the possibility that private indebtedness could bring the world's financial system to the brink of disaster.

Correspondingly, there was no need at all to contemplate that the solvency of parts of the public sector might be questioned once it guaranteed the private debts. So the reaction to the 2007–09 components of the 'private' crisis was focused on resolving problems arising from the private sector. As an example, Para 181 of the De Larosière Group Report in early 2009 states:

> *"Depending on the nature of the risks detected, a proper action has to be taken by the relevant EU authorities. Different types of actions could be required. For example:*
>
> - *If credit expansion appeared to become excessive…*
> - *If the issue is more related to a global dysfunction of the system (e.g. too high maturity transformation, abuse of off-balance sheet transactions, abuse of regulatory arbitrage by non-banks…*
> - *If the concerns were related to fiscal matters (e.g. excesive deficits or the accumulation of debt), the ESRC would immediately relate to the EFC."*

If there was excessive private credit expansion or a structural dysfunction, then there was a lengthy set of detailed solutions. If the problem were rooted in fiscal excesses, the ball should be knocked straight back to the political authorities!

Unfortunately, a year after the De Larosière Group Report, the political authorities were shown to have 'dropped the ball' in Greece over many years – even if the final step was due to the extraordinary accounting practices revealed in the Commission's report of January 2010. However, the Greek crisis has demonstrated the genuine capacity of a public finance crisis to damage the monetary union – even perhaps fatally – because the citizens of Europe have no desire to pay off the profligacies of other EU citizens.

Implementing the de Larosière proposals for supervisory reform: ensnared in both a constitutional and fiscal crisis?

The de Larosière Group (DLG) was created in late 2008 to respond to the turmoil in the private financial markets – then at its height. The European Union has moved rapidly to turn these concepts into legislative reality so that the new supervisory system will be operating from January 2011. But an extra crisis has intruded since then – government debt. So the 2009 Commission proposal is suffering from a transformation to deal with a new crisis. Simultaneously, it became caught in the middle of yet another constitutional power struggle between the Parliament and Council.

The DLG proposed a structure that included a macro-prudential oversight body – European Systemic Risk Board (ESRB) – and a set of micro-prudential bodies. The European System of Financial Supervisors (ESFS) consists of a network of national financial supervisors that deal with supervision of individual firms, working in tandem with the new European Supervisory Authorities (ESAs). There is one ESA for each sector – banking, securities/asset management and insurance/pensions.

The ESRB was originally conceived to sound alerts if credit bubbles were appearing but that seems unlikely to be a problem in the next few years. A second task was to observe any disfunctioning of the financial system. The DLG also proposed that any concerns about fiscal matters would be referred to the political authorities but even that weak formulation disappeared in the Commission plans. But ECON voted that "the ESRB should be empowered not only to warn of an imminent emergency in the economy, but also to declare its existence."

The Commission proposed in September 2009 that the ESAs retain the existing functions of CESR/CEBS/CEIOPS and add the following:

- The ability to develop proposals for technical standards;
- The ability to resolve cases of disagreement between national supervisors, where legislation requires them to co-operate or to agree;
- The power to contribute to ensuring consistent application of technical Community rules (including through peer reviews);
- The European Securities and Markets Authority will exercise direct supervisory powers for Credit Rating Agencies;
- A co-ordination role in emergency situations.

ECOFIN Council responded in December 2009 by eviscerating these proposed powers by leaving only the actual power to impose "binding mediation" – though that is still a significant transfer of powers to the EU level.

The European Parliament's ECON committee voted – in the same week of May 2010 as the Greek component of the crisis reached a peak – to beef up the Commission's plans. It would:

- "Base all the proposed supervisory bodies in Frankfurt and make them part of a tightly-integrated system, replacing the looser network of supervisors in various European cities."
- "Give new powers, such as the possibility of drawing up draft regulatory financial standards which could then be made legally binding by the European Commission. They would also be able to address decisions with legal effect to supervisory authorities that do not conform to EU laws."

- "The committee text also creates a power to supervise directly systemically-important cross-border financial institutions, whereby national supervisors would act as agents of the EU authority."
- "Institutions directly supervised at EU level would be obliged to contribute to a European deposit guarantee fund and a European stability fund."
- "The committee text considerably reduces the latitude for a Member State to invoke the 'safeguard clause' that allows it to avoid implementing a decision of one of the bodies if it considers that the decision creates budgetary problems. The text would require the Member State to provide much clearer proof than had been previously proposed by the Commission and the Council as to how the body's decision creates budgetary problems for it."

Agreement was reached by the co-legislators in September 2010. Finally, the 'supervisory package' was agreed between Council and Parliament – after an epic struggle. But that battle obscured the fact that the EU responded to the crisis with far-reaching changes to its regulatory structure in less than two years from the appointment of the DLG to consider the options.

Moreover, the new co-legislator powers of the Parliament were used to prevent the Council from watering down the proposals, to the point that a citizen could easily ask what changes had been made that corresponded to the magnitude of the problem that had been conclusively demonstrated. On the two counts of speed and constitutional flexibility, the EU can be pleased with the outcome. But we will have to await the judgment of future historians to know if the real test – will the arrangements work in a crisis – will be passed.

So the new 'watchdogs' will be operational from 1 January 2011 – with more or less the powers proposed by the DLG, at

Parliament's insistence. Moreover, the triennial review means that the development process may not yet be finished and Parliament succeeded in enhancing its influence in several key areas.

However, the central importance of the single market also re-emerged powerfully in this debate. As Article 30 of the ESRB Regulation put it: "The establishment of the ESRB should contribute directly to achieving the objectives of the internal market... By addressing such risks, the ESRB should contribute directly to an integrated Union supervisory structure necessary to promote timely and consistent policy responses among the Member States, thus preventing diverging approaches and improving the functioning of the internal market."

So the integration of a single financial market emerges as a critical factor: should the EU move towards 'more Europe or less' in this field? By coincidence, former Commissioner Mario Monti published his report on a 'new strategy for the single market' in the middle of the crisis. He argued that "The single market for capital and the closely interrelated single market for financial services are critical for the efficient allocation of resources – a key driver of growth and employment – and for the stability of the economy." He pointed out that the EU is already committed to far-reaching reform as part of the G20 process and said: "It would be a serious strategic mistake if the Council... were to favour timid solutions." In the end, the co-legislators adopted reasonably bold measures. The apparently technical constraints flowing from the maintenance of the single (or internal) market were analysed in Part I to illustrate the massive economic restraints on political choices that now exist.

May–October 2010: the European fiscal crisis erupts

'Europe' was in crisis and the results will eventually be profound for the relationship of nearly 500 million people (and 22% of world GDP) with the rest of the world. The euro may only be 10 years old, but it is the direct result of a political process that began soon after World War II. It is almost exactly 60 years ago that the then French foreign minister Schuman made his famous Declaration (quoted in the Introduction).

The "concrete achievements" since then include the creation of a single market in 1992 and then the introduction of the euro as the single currency for most EU members in 1999. When financial commentators talk glibly about the possible disintegration of the euro, they may not be thinking deeply about the full implications if such a process were accompanied by a fracturing of this carefully nurtured relationship between France and Germany. There is an alternative outcome to a fracturing: could the crisis instead lead to a deepening of the relationship that would run well beyond France and Germany and include all members of the eurozone?

The crisis has developed far beyond the problems triggered by importing securities backed by sub-prime US mortgages. However, that did precipitate a banking crisis that has required a massive back-stop of public spending, and thus debt, to prevent a slide into a lengthy recession. It is that notching up of debt that has illustrated the unresolved tensions about the conduct of economic policy that is now proving so painful and divisive.

Yet EMU was meant to be founded on policies of fiscal caution that were written twenty years ago to prevent exactly this situation happening: a maximum public deficit of 3% of GDP, public debt ratios should be declining to less than 60% and there was a 'no bail-out' rule precisely to remove the risk that Germany would have to pay off the debts of other countries – for example, Greece was often talked about, even at that stage! Despite the good intentions of the founding fathers, a frantic weekend of negotiations in mid-May that concluded by announcing:

> "The Council and the Member States have decided today on a comprehensive package of measures to preserve financial stability in Europe ... we have decided to establish a European stabilisation mechanism. The mechanism is based on ... an intergovernmental agreement of euro area Member States. Its activation is subject to strong conditionality ... euro area Member States stand ready to complement such resources ... guaranteed on a pro rata basis by participating Member States ... up to a volume of €440 billion ... At the same time, the EU will urgently start working on the necessary reforms to complement the existing framework to ensure fiscal sustainability in the euro area.."

The complete stabilisation package included funding from the full 27 members of the European Union as well as the contribution from the 16 members of the euro zone. In addition, funding from the IMF took the total package to the magic 'US$1 trillion' mark – a significant sum by any standards. That sudden change of heart reflected concerns about the deepening financial crisis. Indeed the Financial Times reported that Europe's banks made a desperate appeal for the European Central Bank to buy the bonds of crisis-hit eurozone members. They said "Worried bankers from 47 European groups urged the ECB to become a 'buyer of last resort' of eurozone government bonds to steady markets." On the Monday after the Council decisions, the ECB reversed its previous policy stance and intervened directly in the markets to buy some EU government bonds.

So there must be further proposals on financial regulation that deal with the problem that the ECB was blackmailed into giving liquidity support to banks that were over-exposed to the public debts of Member States that seemed to be falling into difficulty.

The fall-out from the fiscal crisis will cast a long shadow over the EU's financial system in the years ahead.

Economic co-ordination

Has the pressure of the crisis tipped the 330 million people of the eurozone (and 16% of world GDP) into a tighter union? There is much media discussion about the opposite result – some countries leaving the euro. Under the existing Treaty, there is simply no provision for that, so a country would have to leave the EU as well. That would require a unanimous decision of the 27 members to change the Treaty. In the meantime, anxious depositors would have plenty of time to remove their deposits from banks in any states that might leave. The natural and logical consequence of a collapse of all banks in those states may deter politicians from going down that route. Austerity may be preferable – even if unpleasant.

But a watershed does seem to have been crossed as support was offered to Greece in return for a dramatic tightening of fiscal policy – cutting the budget deficit from 14% of GDP to less than 3% in three years – hardly a bail-out in the usual sense of a gift! Spain and Portugal were also obliged to offer further fiscal cuts and Italy felt it prudent to do so as well. Schuman's "de facto solidarity" concept seems to have been fulfilled financially on this occasion but there is a clear price: economic 'co-ordination' within the eurozone that will be toughened up substantially to stop this happening again.

The European Commission quickly proposed a 'European Semester' for economic – not merely fiscal – policy co-ordination. Member States would undertake "early co-ordination at European level as they prepare their national budgets", thus integrating fiscal policies. But there would be more: "beyond fiscal surveillance, it means a broadening of economic surveillance to the prevention of macroeconomic and competitiveness imbalances ... For euro-area Member States it is proposed to upgrade the peer review of macroeconomic imbalances now carried out by the Eurogroup into a structured surveillance framework".

The heart of the problem lies in the loss of competitiveness of some euro Members that were unwilling to recognise that removing the currency constraint meant they had to conduct a wide array of policies (for example on labour market flexibility) that matched their competitors in the euro area – quite apart from globally. All these policies will now be subject to "structured surveillance" by the eurozone – if the members accept the Commission proposals.

For countries such as Greece and Portugal, this loss of competitiveness showed up as current account deficits above 10% of GDP. These had to be financed by both the public and private sectors taking on huge foreign debts that were bound to become unsustainable eventually. It was the holders of those debts who then cried out for protection in the depth of the crisis. The failure of those lenders could well have triggered a further credit contraction in the rest of the eurozone – and thus another downward twist of the economic spiral.

October–December 2010: the fiscal crisis deepens – becoming overtly a eurozone issue

Ireland's economic misfortunes have precipitated far-reaching changes that must cause a major rethink of many core elements of the EU's regulatory framework for eurozone members. The driving force is the belated recognition by eurozone political leaders that the nature of their debts was fundamentally altered when they gave up the power to print money to repay such debts. Given the huge scale of public debts – tripled as a percentage of GDP in the past four decades – markets are now posing an even more fundamental question: will political leaders countenance an even higher degree of solidarity than they agreed as recently as May? The solution to these questions is increasingly a eurozone rather than EU issue – a bifurcation that may well prove to be a turning point of historic significance.

Recognition of the change in the nature of the debts must surely flow through into the details of technical regulations, but it also highlights an historic political development because the interests of eurozone members increasingly diverge from those of non-members. For eurozone members, phrases such as "shall regard their economic policies as a matter of common concern" (Lisbon Treaty, Art 121) have suddenly stopped being innocuous words in a Treaty that few citizens ever read. Instead, they have been transformed into a political reality that has the power to eject governments as electors are forced to confront the practical results.

Issues for holders of government bonds

It is clear that the scale of the crisis has moved beyond denigrating 'speculators'. Conservative, risk-averse investors are now contemplating the implications – formally and suddenly – of unleashing default risk in government debt. What can governments now say to a pension fund holding a government bond approaching maturity when it asks: why should our pensioners reinvest their life savings in a bond from a state that has deep-rooted problems that could lead to default? Consider the treasurer of a conservative bank that will be *obliged* by Basel III to hold a portfolio of government bonds where some could conceivably take a haircut that is likely to exceed the bank's capital buffer, thus ruining the bank?

Solutions to these questions increase the possibility that the debts of eurozone members will manifestly be subject to a credit risk event and suffer a reduction in value. In the language of accounting standards, they would be 'impaired'. Should holders of such debts be forced to recognise that in their accounts – just as they must mark down a commercial loan?

For the hypothetical pension fund that wishes to minimise the risk to its pensioners' living standards, such questions are likely to be deeply disturbing. The conservative, risk-averse response is likely to be that principal repayments will be reinvested in bonds that, after the 2013 introduction of collective action clauses (CACs), will be issued by prudent governments. They would have a sound fiscal position and no obvious problems of lost competitiveness, political discord etc. which might suddenly risk default in the years ahead.

Investors have learnt to their cost that 'facts' can change with astounding rapidity. In 2006, Ireland was toasted as the AAA Celtic Tiger with a public debt ratio of only 25% of GDP and a fiscal surplus of 3% of GDP. Just four years later, an overblown banking system had ruined the whole country and left government bondholders in despair. It is easy for bondholders to draw up lists of states with some combination of high public debts, poor competitiveness, oversized banking system etc.

Governments outside the prudent group may have to pay an uncomfortably high price for funding, and thus risk a destabilising rise in their interest costs if their public debts are high. Investors do not need to wait until 2013 to foresee these possibilities. Indeed those banks which are seeking to meet the Basel III standards for 2016–18 may already be acting to reach them quickly. Why would they hold bonds of countries that could suffer problems after 2013? They have the word of finance ministers that pre-2013 debtholders have nothing to fear. However these ministers are part of the very institution that permitted Europe to get so over-indebted in the first place. So why should such ministers be trusted?

Is it right that the regulatory framework governing all types of financial institution in the EU should continue with the fiction that debts of EU-penalised governments are risk free and that they are suitable, readily-marketable assets in which banks should hold their liquidity? In Basel III, the global banking supervisors continue to permit this now self-evident fiction. The Irish have just sent a torpedo into the middle of the Basel III concepts. At the very least, the Eurogroup must act together to change EU regulations to take proper account of the new reality they are imposing.

If the answer to such questions is increasingly that conservative investors decide to take any repayments of principal and invest the proceeds in a safer state, then a full-scale 'run' on much sovereign debt is already underway.

Political evolution or revolution: collective decisions by the eurozone?

The fear of such a run drove EU leaders in May to accept far-reaching changes to economic governance, and especially for eurozone members. In September, the European Commission fleshed out the concepts with a package of six detailed proposals that "will integrate all revised and new surveillance processes into a comprehensive and effective economic policy framework." It included "A regulation on the effective enforcement of budgetary surveillance in the euro area", and many provisions of the proposals apply to eurozone members only. Indeed, voting on sanctions will be restricted to such members.

In the context of the EU's normal decision-making process, these evolutionary steps are both radical and extraordinarily rapid. But if a genuine 'run' out of government debt is indeed developing, then revolutionary change may be close at hand.

28 November: At the technical level, the separation between the eurozone and 'other EU members' surfaced even more pointedly in the Irish agreements that day. The Eurogroup, rather than ECOFIN, announced that "Rules will be adapted ... to send a clear signal to private creditors that their claims are subordinated to those of the official sector". Moreover, "Eurogroup Ministers will make a unanimous decision on providing assistance." They also decided that identical collective actions clauses (CAC) will be included in "all new euro area government bonds starting in June 2013" to enable creditors to accept a legally binding change in terms – including haircuts.

Changing the Treaty: The Eurogroup had concluded that some of its members might get into a situation where they do not pay the interest and principal on their loans in a timely fashion – thus accepting that a credit risk can crystallise. Moreover, President van Rompuy "indicated that his proposal on limited Treaty change to the European Council ... will reflect today's decision." The May 2010 credit facilities had three components: IMF, Eurozone members and EU members. The EU members' funding was authorised under Article 122:

1. Without prejudice to any other procedures provided for in the Treaties, the Council, on a proposal from the Commission, may decide, in a spirit of solidarity between Member States, upon the measures appropriate to the economic situation, in particular if severe difficulties arise in the supply of certain products, notably in the area of energy.
2. Where a Member State is in difficulties or is seriously threatened with severe difficulties caused by natural disasters or exceptional occurrences beyond its control, the Council, on a proposal from the Commission, may grant, under certain conditions, Union financial assistance to the Member State concerned. The President of the Council shall inform the European Parliament of the decision taken.

But that raised a number of questions:

- If the proposed recipient of the assistance has failed to follow Eurogroup advice – even to the point of suffering sanctions – that State can hardly be said to be acting in a spirit of solidarity. So it ought not to be eligible for assistance.
- If the crisis is the natural, logical consequence of its own actions, then it may be difficult to argue that the events are "beyond its control". It now seems Greece's national accounts misled the rest of the EU. Irish commentators are increasingly discussing the nexus between politicians, property developers and bankers.
- When ECOFIN has so strikingly failed to find the courage to discipline its members, the European Parliament may not be willing to agree to a Treaty change that continues this failed system. It may want to be involved more than merely being "informed". That could go beyond the current proposal of increased 'automaticity': Commission proposals are accepted unless they are overturned by a qualified majority of Member States.
- Will non-eurozone states be willing to fund such loans? For the UK, the answer seems to be explicit – no. So the Heads of Government decided that Article 122 would no longer be used as the legal basis for funding eurozone members.

December 15: Another solution seemed necessary and the European Parliament warned against deciding the bail-out mechanism details in back-room, late-night deals among Member States. It argued that Parliament must be closely involved, to ensure the mechanism's accountability, transparency and legitimacy vis-à-vis markets and citizens. The mechanism's details should instead be proposed by the Commission, and negotiated by Parliament and the Council, it said. Furthermore, the bail-out mechanism must be strongly linked to forthcoming legislation setting up a new economic governance model, it added. The resolution called for great attention to clarity on a number of issues, arguing that otherwise it will be difficult to ensure stability.

It also argued that private sector participation in any burden-sharing should be handled on a case-by-case basis, and called on the Commission to present a comprehensive description of how investors, savers and market participants will be involved and state explicitly that the mechanism will be fully consistent with IMF policy regarding private sector involvement.

December 17: The Heads of Government decided to add an extra clause to Article 136: "3. The Member States whose currency is the euro may establish a stability mechanism to be activated if indispensable to safeguard the stability of the euro area as a whole. The granting of any required financial assistance under the mechanism will be made subject to strict conditionality." So the eurozone, rather than the whole EU, was to be responsible for dealing with all future ramifications of this crisis.

Prior to the additional clause, Article 136 ran as follows:

1 In order to ensure the proper functioning of economic and monetary union, and in accordance with the relevant provisions of the Treaties, the Council shall, in accordance with the relevant procedure from among those referred to in Articles 121 and 126, with the exception of the procedure set out in Article 126(14), adopt measures specific to those Member States whose currency is the euro: (a) to strengthen the co-ordination and surveillance of their budgetary discipline; (b) to set out economic policy guidelines for them, while ensuring that they are compatible with those adopted for the whole of the Union and are kept under surveillance.

2 For those measures set out in paragraph 1, only members of the Council representing Member States whose currency is

the euro shall take part in the vote. A qualified majority of the said members shall be defined in accordance with Article 238(3)(a).

After the December 17 Summit: still waiting for the real decisions

This Treaty revision was formulated as a deft constitutional measure to sidestep the need for an Inter-Governmental Conference (IGC) and a referendum in Ireland. In choosing this route, the Heads of Government ruled out a more substantial Treaty revision that would be necessary to permit any of the fashionable ideas of 'Euro-bonds' or 'E-bonds'. Such concepts would almost certainly fall foul of Article 125 "The Union shall not be liable for or assume the commitments of central government…". Changing that article would represent an unmistakable transfer of power so would require a full IGC to prepare the way – taking a year or more. But the resulting Treaty change would require referenda in Ireland and Denmark. The UK is now well advanced into the process of enacting a European Union Bill that would impose referenda in the UK on all but the most minor Treaty changes.

The chances of a Treaty change being agreed and ratified within the timescale of a rapidly rising fiscal crisis are close to nil. Practical solutions to this crisis must be found within existing institutional arrangements. In the decades ahead, the eurozone may prove that its collective economic governance arrangements really do force its members to pursue fiscally sound policies, so adopting joint liabilities could well be non-controversial at that stage.

Regrettably, the December 17 solution was not crafted by statesmen with a clear vision of how to solve the euro's crisis. So the Heads of Government may be forced to return to the problem early in 2011.

Their finance ministers agreed in November on the formulation of the European Stability Mechanism (ESM) – based on the European Financial Stability Fund (EFSF) – to complement the enhanced economic surveillance that has been agreed in May. The ESM will take effect in 2013 and its creditor status will rank below IMF loans but ahead of the private sector.

Private lenders should have no doubt about their vulnerability after 2013. Indeed, all the 'problem' countries – measured by elevated credit spreads – plan to have a primary surplus by then, so the financial markets will only be needed to fund interest payments due be paid back to the markets themselves. These states plan to issue nearly €350 billion of bonds in 2011, with about half that intended to refinance maturities. It is those refinancings that may force Heads of Government to meet again in agonised conclaves.

However, the eurozone Heads of Government – *not* the heads of all EU governments – did make a powerful statement at the Summit. It is that spirit that seems to have infused the New Year message of Chancellor Merkel and President Sarkozy.

Statement by the Heads of State or Government of the euro area and the EU institutions

The Heads of State or Government of the euro area and the EU institutions have made it clear, as set out below, *that they stand ready to do whatever is required to ensure the stability of the euro area as a whole. The euro is and will remain a central part of European integration* [author's emphasis]. In particular, the Heads called for determined action in the following areas:

a) Fully implementing existing programmes: we welcome the impressive progress made in implementing the Greek programme and the agreed adjustment programme for Ireland, including the adoption of the 2011 budget.
b) Keeping up fiscal responsibility: we are all committed to strictly implementing the budgetary policy recommendations, fully respecting the fiscal targets for 2010 and 2011 and to correcting excessive deficits within the agreed deadlines.
c) Stepping up growth enhancing structural reforms: we are determined to accelerate structural reforms to enhance growth.
d) Strengthening the Stability and Growth Pact and implementing a new macro-surveillance framework from summer 2011.
e) Ensuring the availability of adequate financial support through the EFSF pending the entry into force of the permanent mechanism: we note that only a very limited amount has been committed from the EFSF to support the Irish programme.
f) Further strengthening of the financial system both as regards the regulatory and supervisory frameworks and conducting new stress tests in the banking sector.
g) Expressing full support to ECB action: we support the ECB in its independent responsibility to ensure price stability, solidly anchor inflation expectations and thereby contribute to financial stability of the euro area. We are committed to ensuring the financial independence of the central banks of the Eurosystem. Elements of this strategy will be further developed in the coming months as a comprehensive response to any challenges, as part of our new economic governance.

Part III

Why financial integration will force political integration in 2011 and later

Searching finance

European government bonds in 2011

Consider the choices facing a pension fund manager whose fund receives the redemption money into a bank account at a global SIFI that is clearly too-big-to-fail. Should he leave it there with near-absolute certainty that the money will still be available for the pension payment schedule that is known with complete certainty for 10 years' time? Or should he reinvest it in the 10-year bonds of State X where there is a real question of a partial default (known as a 'haircut') at the end of the term. The fund manager will probably still be in his job at that time and be fully accountable to the pensioners. He can tell them that he had the word of a group of finance ministers in 2010 that the bonds issued in 2011 would be safe. But the impoverished pensioners might retort that such ministers had collectively signed pieces of paper for many years and made speeches about prudent fiscal policy, yet utterly failed to prevent the crisis. Moreover, probably none of them expected to be still in office at the bond's maturity. So the governance of the process was weak.

In 2011, there will be an alternative possibility for the fund manager: invest in the bonds issued by the EFSF that would fund State X if it cannot raise funds in the market – or is unwilling to pay the price, fearing a ruinous interest burden. The EFSF bond will be rated AAA (see below) by the rating agencies the governments dislike so much, but the fund manager will be under a duty to investigate carefully for himself the exact credit mechanics. These will be complex as each issue is backed by a set of guarantees that will vary if any of the guarantors – which include all the other 'problem states' – fall into default themselves. Nonetheless, these EFSF bonds will be senior to any other bonds available and the aggregate guarantees from *all* the other eurozone members will make them reasonably credible. Thus risk-averse, conservative fund managers may gravitate to EFSF bonds rather than funding State X direct.

If problem states do default, Eurostat will allocate the guarantees directly to the balance sheet of the guaranteeing states, so their own indebtedness will rise – reducing the credibility of problem states even further. There is a further twist to this vicious circle. The EU seems to have forgotten the lessons learnt after the Second World War: the Treaty of Versailles in 1918 exacted such reparations from Germany that they ruined the country and led on to political instability. So a founding principle of the EU became 'solidarity'. By charging say Ireland a 6% interest rate, the other eurozone members will be extracting a substantial income above the EFSF's cost of funding. A future, populist Irish government may feel this is unfair, and lacking in solidarity. So the risk of actual default may rise – especially as there will probably be a primary surplus at the time.

Our fund manager will be contemplating all these scenarios that could play out during the life of the bonds to be offered to him in 2011, and be ever more wary of taking the risk of buying direct obligations of any but the safest governments. So the size of the EFSF will have to be raised progressively at crisis meeting after crisis meeting until it is funding many of the problem states entirely.

Economic governance of the eurozone

During the heat of the crisis In May 2010, the EU Heads of Government agreed on the principles of a package of economic measures for "...necessary reforms to complement the existing framework to ensure fiscal sustainability in the euro area..." At the end of June, a Commission Communication laid out more details:

- Developing the proposals for greater economic policy co-ordination and surveillance set out in the Commission's 12 May Communication on reinforcing economic policy co-ordination into concrete proposals by (i) addressing imbalances through stronger macroeconomic surveillance, including alert and sanction mechanisms; (ii) strengthening national fiscal frameworks by specifying minimum requirements for domestic fiscal frameworks, and notably moving from annual to multi-annual budgetary planning; (iii) strengthening the Stability and Growth Pact, in particular by focusing on the issue of debt dynamic as well as deficits;
- Setting out effective enforcement mechanisms to ensure that Member States will act in compliance with the EU framework they have agreed. Where developments in Member State economies pose a risk to the overall development of the Union, a series of preventive and corrective measures are proposed, including a range of sanctions that could be applied where breaches occur;
- Proposing the establishment of a European semester for policy co-ordination. The process and timing are explained. The European Semester will provide a European input to national policy decisions, leading to more effective ex-ante policy co-ordination. This also applies to the structural reforms and the growth-enhancing elements of the Europe 2020 strategy.

In September, the legislative texts were published, and at the December Summit, the Heads of Government *"reiterated our commitment to reach agreement on the legislative proposals on economic governance by end June 2011 with the aim of strengthening the economic pillar of the Economic and Monetary Union…"*

The politics of these proposals are a huge step towards a more collective form of economic governance that will amount to a loose federation once fully operational. The highlighted points in the box below make it very clear that the collective examination run by the Commission will be highly detailed and flow into virtually every aspect of a state's economic life if 'imbalances' begin to appear. Competitiveness covers wide swathe of a nation's economic activity because it goes to the heart of the performance of the entire private sector.

Proposal for a Regulation on enforcement measures to correct excessive macroeconomic imbalances in the Euro Area

[COM(2010) 525/2]

...Overall, it was agreed that macroeconomic surveillance should function alongside the budget surveillance under the Stability and Growth Pact.... The conclusions of the European Council of 16 September 2010 *welcomed the development of a new macro-surveillance framework to monitor and correct unsustainable competitiveness divergences and imbalances* in timely manner.... Possible indicators would most likely include both external and internal ones. Measures of the external position (e.g. current accounts and external debt) and price or cost competitiveness (e.g. real effective exchange rates) would facilitate the detection of external imbalances. The use of internal indicators (e.g. private and public sector debt) is justified on the ground that external imbalances necessarily have internal counterparts. *The monitoring of internal indicators can also be justified on its own sake on the ground that internal imbalances can have repercussions on other Member States, particularly via financial contagion.*

If the in-depth review points to severe imbalances or imbalances that jeopardise the proper functioning of the Economic and Monetary Union in a specific Member State, the Council may, on a recommendation from the Commission, adopt recommendations in accordance with Article 121(4) of the Treaty declaring the existence of an excessive imbalance and recommending the Member State concerned to take corrective action within a specified deadline and to present its policy intentions in a corrective action plan. Member States with excessive imbalances within the meaning of the EIP would be subjected to stepped-up peer pressure. These 'EIP recommendations' should be made public; they should be more detailed and prescriptive than the 'preventive' recommendations provided for in Article 6. *Depending on the nature of the imbalance, the policy prescriptions could potentially address fiscal, wage, macro-structural and macro-prudential policy aspects under the control of government authorities.* [Author's emphasis throughout.]

Nonetheless, examination of the proposal to enforce these mechanisms is likely to leave a bond market investor deeply sceptical about the ability, and even willingness, of eurozone members to exert genuine discipline on a member government that is determined to ignore recommendations for correcting its 'economic imbalance' and the subsequent fiscal deficits that are likely. Two eurozone members have already demonstrated that public finances really can become unsustainable in reality. Few investors would expect the imposition of a yearly fine of 0.1% of GDP to have the slightest effect in *forcing* a government to take serious corrective measures. Yet the likely consequences of such behaviour are made abundantly clear.

A Regulation on enforcement measures to correct excessive macroeconomic imbalances in the Euro Area

Macroeconomic imbalances are likely to generate undue fluctuations in public revenues and spending throughout the economic cycle, affecting headline figures and distorting the picture for fiscal planning and decision-making. Inappropriate fiscal policy choices based on distorted trends could weaken, and possibly compromise, the sustainability of public finances. If unchecked, fiscal and other macroeconomic imbalances have the potential to reinforce each other and possibly to jeopardise the proper functioning of economic and monetary union. For these reasons a system of correction of macroeconomic imbalances should contribute to the budgetary discipline of the Member States whose currency is the euro.

Source: COM (2010) 525/2

The proposals on 'Strengthening the Stability and Growth Pact' (amending Regulation (EC) No 1467/97) seem more promising but the maximum fine remains at 0.5% of GDP. Moreover, the history of ECOFIN does not inspire confidence that such penalties will ever be enforced. This body presided over a rise in public debt ratios from around 60% of GDP at the launch of the euro to nearly 90% currently – without any sanctions ever being imposed at all. It is that decade-long failure that is the root cause of today's problems. However, the chances of penalties being imposed are certainly heightened by the proposal that the Commission's recommendations can only be overturned by a Qualified Majority Vote by Council against the Commission.

How to make sanctions effective

Policymakers must move back to first principles swiftly to ensure that no Member State can ever blackmail the Union again. The approach must be as rigorous and comprehensive as the reforming response to the private sector crisis because the Union has been proven beyond all reasonable doubt to have defective disciplining mechanisms. This is the challenge for 2011.

Examining the Commission's proposed amendments to this Regulation, it might be possible to add paragraphs to Article 12 that would require the ESRB explicitly to opine *in public* on any risks posed to the EU's financial system by a state that was subject to a second year of fines. This would fall naturally within its mission and tasks (see below). If the recommendations for remedial action still go unheeded, then there should be powers within the upcoming fourth revision to the Capital Requirements Directive (CRD IV) to permit the European Banking Authority to remove progressively the special privileges accorded to the debt of this state when held by financial institutions. Perhaps the ESRB could make a specific proposal to the EBA to take this action.

For more details of this approach, see Appendix I: Market Discipline on Eurozone Public Debt – amend SGP Regulation and CRD IV.

Proposed Regulation amendments

[COM(2010) 522]

'Article 11

Whenever the Council decides to apply sanctions to a participating Member State in accordance with Article 126(11) of the Treaty, a fine shall, as a rule, be required. The Council may decide to supplement this fine by the other measures provided for in Article 126(11) of the Treaty.'

'Article 12

1. The amount of the fine shall comprise a fixed component equal to 0.2% of GDP, and a variable component. The variable component shall amount to one tenth of the difference between the deficit as a percentage of GDP in the preceding year and either the reference value for government deficit or, if non compliance with budgetary discipline includes the debt criterion, the general government balance as a percentage of GDP that should have been achieved in the same year according to the notice issued under Article 126(9) of the Treaty.
2. Each following year, until the decision on the existence of an excessive deficit is abrogated, the Council shall assess whether the participating Member State concerned has taken effective action in response to the Council notice in accordance with Article 126(9) of the Treaty. In this annual assessment the Council shall decide, in accordance with Article 126(11) of the Treaty, to intensify the sanctions, unless the participating Member State concerned has complied with the Council notice. If an additional fine is decided, it shall be calculated in the same way as for the variable component of the fine in paragraph 1.
3. Any single fine referred to in paragraphs 1 and 2 shall not exceed the upper limit of 0.5% of GDP.'

The Role of the European Systemic Risk Board (ESRB)

The legislation establishing the European Systemic Risk Board came into force on 16 December 2010 and the inaugural meeting of the General Board of the ESRB is on 20 January 2011. The ESRB is an independent EU body responsible for the macro-prudential oversight of the financial system within the Union.

The De Larosière Group's report originally discussed public finances as a separate topic but the final ESRB Regulation appears to be sufficiently widely drawn that a crisis in the government bond markets should fall within the definitions in Article 2: (b) 'financial system' means all financial institutions, markets, products and market infrastructures; (c) 'systemic risk' means a risk of disruption in the financial system with the potential to have serious negative consequences for the internal market and the real economy.

All types of financial intermediaries, markets and infrastructure may be potentially systemically important to some degree. So these definitions should permit the ESRB to recommend action – given its mission statement.

The ESRB's mission and tasks are laid down in Article 3 of the Regulation:

1 The ESRB shall be responsible for the macro-prudential oversight of the financial system within the Union in order to contribute to the prevention or mitigation of systemic risks to financial stability in the Union that arise from developments within the financial system and taking into account macroeconomic developments, so as to avoid periods of widespread financial distress. It shall contribute to the smooth functioning of the internal market and thereby ensure a sustainable contribution of the financial sector to economic growth.

2 For the purposes of paragraph 1, the ESRB shall carry out the following tasks: (a) determining and/or collecting and analysing all the relevant and necessary information, for the purposes of achieving the objectives described in paragraph 1; (b) identifying and prioritising systemic risks; (c) issuing warnings where such systemic risks are deemed to be significant and, where appropriate, making those warnings public; (d) issuing recommendations for remedial action in response

to the risks identified and, where appropriate, making those recommendations public.

As ESRB Chairman Jean-Claude Trichet put it in November "On the question of 'how' to do macro-prudential oversight, the main tools that the ESRB will have at its disposal are warnings and recommendations. As we know, the strength of the so-called 'soft law' can be quite significant, notwithstanding the lack of direct enforcement power. When risks have been identified and appear to be large, the ESRB will issue precise risk warnings. When appropriate, it will complement warnings with recommendations for remedial action and indications of the risks of inaction. We assume that the addressees will give careful consideration to the measures the ESRB will propose.

"I am confident that the ESRB will quickly develop its credibility through its work, its warnings and its recommendations. Its authority will draw on the quality of its analysis and its deep understanding of the functioning of the financial sector." At its first meeting on 20 January, the ESRB should be able to get down to the serious business of considering the systemic risks that may well flow from the risk aversions implied by the current pattern of government bond yields.

European Financial Stability Fund (EFSF)

On 21 December, the funding plans to support Ireland were announced:

- The Eurogroup and the EU's Council of Economics and Finance Ministers had decided on 28 November 2010 to grant financial assistance in response to the Irish authorities' request. The financial package will cover financing needs up to €85 billion. The EU will provide up to €22.5 billion and the EFSF up to €17.7 billion over 2011 and 2012.
- In the first quarter of 2011, the EU (under the auspices of the EFSM) and the EFSF will disburse €11.7 billion to

Ireland in total. Subsequent disbursements are subject to quarterly reviews.

- In 2011 the EU will, under auspices of the EFSM, raise up to €17.6 billion and in 2012 up to €4.9 billion. Based on these amounts, subject to revision and Ireland's requirements, the EU intends to launch in 2011 four to five benchmark bonds aiming at €3 to €5 billion for each transaction. The EU may complement its funding needs by smaller bond issues, either through taps of issues launched under the EFSM or targeted transactions. In the first half of 2011 the market should expect three EU benchmark transactions.
- The EFSF in 2011 will raise funds up to €16.5 billion and in 2012 up to €10 billion. It intends, also subject to revision, to launch next year three benchmark bonds aiming at €3 to €5 billion for each transaction.

The EU and the EFSF are rated AAA by the three major rating agencies, Fitch, Moody's and Standard & Poor's. The extract below sets out Moody's rating rationale. There is an irony that the EU Member States have to pay such attention to the rating agencies just at a time when they are trying to find ways to reduce their influence in financial regulations more generally. However, the complexity of the EFSF's issues illustrates the efficiency gains to the market as a whole in having a small number of independent players monitor these arrangement, rather than literally thousands of European banks, insurers and UCIT mangers each making their own analysis.

The rating analysis demonstrated that if a rising number of eurozone states have to be funded by the EFSF, then the guarantees that fall on the AAA countries will be substantial. Moreover, the European Council decided in December that 'Article 122' loans by the EU as a whole would not be made for this purpose in future, so the full burden of any additional borrowers will fall on the EFSF.

Moody's rating rationale

The (P)Aaa rating is based on EFSF's contractual elements, including the irrevocable and unconditional guarantees by the participating states, EFSF's cash reserve and the loan-specific cash buffer as well as the creditworthiness of the participating Aaa Eurozone Member States and their firm commitment to EFSF.

Each loan to a member state will be funded by a debt issuance by the EFSF. The debt issuance will be used to fund the loan, the EFSF cash reserve and a loan-specific cash buffer which represents an additional cash set-aside to support repayment of the debt. At the same time, all member states participating in the EFSF program but not borrowing from the program will provide a 120% guarantee of the entire EFSF debt issue, apportioned by their respective shares in the European Central Bank's capital.

The loan-specific cash buffer will be sized so that the remaining portion of the debt issue that is not fully backed cash will be fully covered by Aaa-rated member states.

"As a result, each EFSF debt issuance is backed first by the promise to repay the loan by the borrowing member state, then by Aaa-rated guarantees and cash sufficient by themselves to cover all of associated debt service if the loan is not repaid, plus guarantees from the non-Aaa rated members states participating in the EFSF support program," explains Dietmar Hornung, Vice President – Senior Credit Officer in Moody's Sovereign Risk Group.

Risks that could negatively affect the creditworthiness of a programme after its issuance include a potential deterioration in the creditworthiness of the participating Eurozone Member States. Changes in the ratings of these countries could result in downward pressure on ratings assigned to EFSF issuances.

The creditworthiness of issuance programmes would be particularly sensitive to changes in the ratings of Aaa countries with large EFSF contribution keys, i.e. Germany, France, and the Netherlands. Moreover, a weakening of the Eurozone Member States' commitment to EFSF could have negative rating implications.

The following credit enhancements are in place:

- Over-guarantee mechanism: Each guarantor is required to issue an irrevocable and unconditional guarantee which in aggregate amounts to an overall 120% over-guarantee of the obligations of the EFSF (principal and interest) in respect of the funding instruments issued or entered into by the EFSF. Hence, each Eurozone Member State issues a capped guarantee in proportion to its share in the ECB capital, leading to guarantees that exceed the value of the issued debt by 20%. If a supporting state becomes a borrower, it may – if all guarantors agree – step out as a guarantor although this would not affect its liability under existing guarantees.
- EFSF cash reserve:
- Loan-specific cash buffer: In addition to the cash reserve, every time the EFSF makes a loan under a loan facility agreement to a borrower member state, it will establish a loan-specific cash buffer which will be sized such that each EFSF loan is fully covered by Aaa guarantees and/or an amount of cash equal to the relevant portion of the EFSF cash reserve plus any loan-specific cash buffer.

Potential additional support: While a pure quantitative analysis of the contractual arrangements per se supports the assignment of a (P)Aaa rating, the downgrade risk of a programme after its issuance is mitigated by the strong implicit support for this facility evident among the participating countries. Statements by the

Eurozone Members' respective heads of state reflect the high-level commitment to EFSF.

Nevertheless, a default on EFSF debt would entail significant pecuniary and political costs for Europe. "Apart from threatening the survival of the European Monetary Union, it would also result in considerable reputational risks for core European countries like Germany and France, and would likely increase their borrowing costs," says Mr. Hornung.

In the event that the existing contractual credit enhancements proved insufficient to EFSF debt service requirements, additional support from the Eurozone Member States would likely be sought.

Timetable for first half of 2011

As markets get back into their stride at the beginning of 2011, it seems that six eurozone states are now regarded by markets as 'risky' – defined as having 10-year bond spread that are more than 100bp above German yields. The markets now include Belgium in the risky category. In the first months of the year they will be issuing collectively more than €30 billion each month. Funding planned for the EU and EFSF to pass on to both Ireland and Greece looks set to be around a third of that. But that will be sufficiently large – especially with benchmark issues – to generate noticeable competition for the 'risky' sovereigns as both the EU and EFSF will be AAA-rated. The possibility that conservative investors will shun one or more of the risky states in favour of the AAA rated issuers could be a subject for the ESRB's inaugural meeting as such a development could trigger a vicious circle.

The table below also includes the currently scheduled legislative meetings of the Parliament and Council – though additional meetings can be arranged at short notice! If the Heads of Government really want to convince markets that the economic governance issues have been settled by the end of June, then there is a very tight timetable for both ECOFIN and ECON to respond to the Commission proposals and agree on a compromise in a Single Reading.

Already ECB President Trichet has appealed to MEPs to play the card of ambition to reform the Commission's proposals on economic governance which, "although going in the right direction, lack some boldness and detail". In a veiled criticism of recent events, Trichet repeatedly took the opportunity to call for "verbal discipline and clarity" which was essential in such times. "As co-legislators on this package I have no doubt that you will be up to the challenge of making the economic governance model better."

Parliament's Rapporteur Ms Corien Wortman-Kool welcomed the proposed strengthening of the SGP and demanded a strong role for the Commission in applying its rules, which provide inter alia for sanctions against governments that do not abide by the principles of prudent fiscal policy making. "If Member States in the Council decide, the risk is that the debate will be highly politicised", she warned. Parliament's initial comments are already substantially more ambitious for a European dimension than the Commission proposals. The draft reports are scheduled be presented in committee on 24 and 25 January 2011.

So the backdrop to a series of potentially difficult bond issues by risky states will be a string of rows among EU policymakers that may make market participants wonder about how serious the Member States really are about preventing any recurrence of this type of fiscal crisis. Despite the measure already taken, the Commission's autumn forecasts still point to rising debt burdens this year and next in the risky states – in some case quite sharply. Only in Italy is stability expected.

Currently scheduled legislative meetings of the Parliament and Council

2011	'Risky' bond issues, €bn	EFSF + EU issues, €bn		Meetings		
		Ireland	Greece	ESRB	Parliament	Council
Jan	35		6.5	20th	10th + 24/25th ECON	17/18th Eurogroup/ECOFIN
Feb	33	11.7			1st + 7th ECON	4th – European Council 14/15th Eurogroup/ECOFIN
Mar	30		10.9	??	15/16th + 21-23rd ECON	15th ECOFIN 24/25th European Council
April	25					7/8th Informal ECOFIN
May	23	3?				17th ECOFIN
June	34		8.7			15th ECOFIN 24th European Council

Note: Risky = eurozone governments with 10 year bond yields > 100bp above Germany on 04/01/2011

Three scenarios for the future of the eurozone

The eurozone now faces several options for its future actions. Considering specific scenarios may be the best mechanism to illustrate the choices that must be made and each scenario below simply lays out the developments that flow logically after each choice.

Scenario I: inflationary debt spiral

1. EFSF initial issues well received as investors only want to fund risky states with guarantees from other eurozone members and minimum risk of partial defaults (haircuts).
2. Subsequent failure of a risky state auction as funds siphoned off to EFSF.
3. Emergency meeting of Heads of Government to increase size of EFSF.
4. France and Germany carry through the commitments implied in their New Year messages (and statement at December Summit) but only grudgingly agree to the minimum ceiling need to accommodate the state whose auction has just failed.
5. The next domino falls shortly after.
6. Repeat steps 4 and 5 until EFSF guarantee matrix has become utterly incomprehensible.
7. Meanwhile ECOFIN eviscerates the Commission's already weak economic governance proposals – making clear to investors that, collectively, the eurozone governments are unwilling to enforce serious fiscal discipline.
8. Flight of capital from eurozone; short- and long-term interest rates rise significantly; investors quickly realise that the extra interest costs will add another 2–3 % of GDP on to budget

deficits and that a debt spiral is now locked in with high, imported inflation.

Scenario II: default

1 EFSF initial issues well received as investors only want to fund risky states with guarantees from other eurozone members and minimum risk of partial defaults (haircuts).
2 Subsequent failure of a risky state auction as funds siphoned off to fund EFSF.
3 Emergency meeting of Heads of Government.
4 France and Germany carry through the commitments implied in their New Year messages (and statement at December Summit) to increase the size of EFSF to give a ceiling that accommodates all issuance of risky states for three years.
5 ECOFIN and Parliament move swiftly to agree an economic governance package that goes well beyond the Commission proposals.
6 Despite the repeated commitments by all eurozone members since May 2010, a risky State holds out against the tough proposals and penal interest rates, is voted down and subjected to sanctions which it ignores.
7 Investors decline to fund new loans to it and it declares default as it is now in primary surplus so only needs new loans to pay interest to the market. The dominos fall in other risky states.
8 Aghast, the Heads of Government contemplate the domino effects and consider the BIS data for lending by their banks. The Heads of Government for Austria, France, Germany and Netherlands find that their banks have made 23% (June 2010) of their loans to borrowers in the six risky states – a cash sum of €1.9 trillion.
9 These losses vastly exceed their banks' capital. Widespread nationalisation ensues of many banks in these member states given the losses on the supposedly risk-free bonds that they

were obliged to purchase by regulatory requirements, as well as private sector loans that now default. For France and Germany, taking these doubtful bank assets onto the national balance sheet pushes their own debt ratios above 100% of GDP.

10 Some members leave the EU and recreate their own currencies – with large and overtly competitive devaluations. Public fury at their betrayal by their partners quickly leads to a breakdown of the single market and any sense of political unity. The EU ceases to operate as an organised political system.

11 What next?

Scenario III: a collectively strong, federal 'Eurozone' emerges

1 EFSF issues not well received as private investors distrust the complex guarantee system, given the expected domino effects of risky states.

2 Emergency meeting of Heads of Government.

3 France and Germany carry through the commitments implied in their New Year messages (and statement at December Summit: *"that they stand ready to do whatever is required to ensure the stability of the euro area as a whole."*) What will be required is that they increase the size of the EFSF to give a ceiling that accommodates all public debt issuance of risky states for long enough to prove that the economic and fiscal policies to be enacted during the 'European Semester' in early 2011 are working in practice.

4 Investors can readily calculate that the risky states may need gross funding of around €1 trillion in the next three years. As Commissioner Olli Rehn put it in his FT article (11 January 2011), "The national reform programmes that EU member states are preparing will push forward these reforms. But there is insufficient ambition and a lack of urgency in imple-

mentation. That needs to change before the programmes are finalised in April."

5 The March European Council has its now-normal sub-meeting of Eurozone members and concludes that it is indeed in their best interest to avoid a collapse of the euro and that they have no economic, political or historical option except to "do whatever is required". So it lays down that:

a The 'programmes' must be sufficiently rigorous that they will meet any requirement of tough conditionality for EFSF loans and are acceptable to the IMF.

b The size of the EFSF will be increased so that under any plausible scenario it can disburse €1 trillion in cash. Under the existing system of guarantees and cash collateral, that could require a virtual quadrupling of the nominal size. (Governments had realised that the actual banking liabilities that could fall on them under Scenario II might be much larger – perhaps even twice the sum they need to be able to disburse.)

c The EFSF's own funding costs will be passed through to the borrowers as an act of solidarity rather than meanness. That will encourage risky states to request EFSF funding at an early stage rather than waiting until disaster is at hand because it will be cheaper and without stigma as the state will already have voluntarily agreed to the terms as part of its programme.

6 Eurozone governments mount a major education programme to inform their electors of the unpalatable truth of the situation and electors understand this is the best outcome available.

7 'Risky government' bonds begin to rally sharply as fears of imminent default dissipate.

8 At the end of March, the new European Banking Authority starts the 2011 round of stress tests of European banks. With

these new arrangements in place, it states that banks do not need to make provisions against Eurozone government bonds held in their 'banking book'. Investors accept this argument is now credible. (In 2010, they did *not* accept its credibility, so the fear of a cover-up inflamed market concerns rather than cooled them. Market players feared then that the implicit guarantors of the banking system did not know how big their potential liabilities were and if they did, knew they could not meet them.) ECOFIN and Parliament move *in parallel* with that EFSF expansion and swiftly agree an economic governance package that goes well beyond the Commission proposals, giving certainty to the 'bond market vigilantes' that this type of fiscal crisis will not happen again because Eurozone is genuinely in charge and flanking policy measures on financial regulation ensure that the banking system cannot become so overexposed.

9 The decisions of the March Eurozone Council meeting make it clear that the EFSF effectively has become a joint and several guarantee mechanism for those eurozone members that are in fact resolving their individual fiscal problems, together with tough collective oversight to confirm that the 'strong conditionality' is being followed through.

10 Eurozone becomes somewhat introverted in order to concentrate on the pressing economic needs of its 330 (and rising) million citizens. There is not time to consider the interests of non-members – such as 60 million Britons.

11 After a year or two, the effects of the drive to enhance Eurozone's competitiveness begin to come through, and its public finances improve sharply.

12 Any bonds of the risky states that remain outstanding seem very attractive – to those investors able to buy them. The potential wave of defaults is likely to have precipitated a further round of regulatory reform to ensure that financial

institutions such as banks will find it difficult to buy bonds of any but the soundest states. That will be a major constraint on finance ministers ever getting into such debts again.

13 Risk premia dwindle steadily as public finances improve and the euro rises, reducing the risk of importing inflation. No EFSF guarantees are actually called as markets are again willing to fund all eurozone members. But most states continue to find it cheaper to fund themselves via the EFSF as it has also built up a critical mass as one of the world's most liquid bond markets. Moreover, the credit quality is now seen as outstanding, given Eurozone's institutionalised, intrusive oversight of competitiveness and fiscal probity. International investors recognise that this policy constraint is more effective in Eurozone than in alternative global bond markets.

14 Eurozone has now emerged from the financial crisis as a political federation – loose in some respects, but with tightly centralised economic governance at its heart.

The visionary approach shown under Scenario III matches the sense of history demonstrated after the Second World War and that is why the leaders of Eurozone will rise to the occasion. Moreover, they stared into an economic and political abyss without parallel in modern times and had little choice but to follow the route that gave a reasonable possibility of a good outcome.

(It should be noted that the historical timeline of this analysis started with Churchill's post-war encouragement of a Franco-German union as the solution to a massive economic and political crisis. It would be interesting to consider what he would have said about the UK absenting itself from the field at the critical time after he had proposed the political solution of a complete Franco-British Union in a moment of crisis 70 years ago.)

Appendix I: Market Discipline on Eurozone Public Debt – amend SGP Regulation and CRD IV

The role of market discipline on fiscal excesses in a monetary union was examined in Graham Bishop's writings from 1990–93. These papers were controversial during the Maastricht Treaty negotiations as they doubted the willingness of finance ministers to discipline profligate states. The principal papers are listed in Appendix II.

Market Discipline on Eurozone Public Debt

The outlook for public debt is being questioned to the extent that it is now necessary to add a provision in CRD IV that would apply higher capital requirements and limit 'large exposures' for banks lending to eurozone Member States that fail to implement Excessive Deficit Procedure (EDP) recommendations by Council. This can be structured so there is a progressive reduction in the EU banking system's exposure to a deteriorating state.

A policy along these lines could be implemented quickly as the only requirements would be a change in the Regulations setting up the SGP; appropriate language in CRD IV and corresponding changes in other sectoral legislation – just as the Omnibus Directive is doing for the creation of the European Supervisory Authorities (ESAs). The changes may sound modest, but they would be profound in protecting the European Union from the all-too-apparent risk of fiscal crises as the baby-boomers move into an expensive old-age.

Background

The role of market discipline on fiscal excesses in a monetary union was examined in Graham Bishop's writings from 1990–93. These papers (see Appendix II) were controversial during the Maastricht Treaty negotiations as they doubted the willingness of finance ministers to discipline profligate states. Eventually, financial markets would not lend citizen's retirement savings to such states so banking regulations should be amended to preclude the risk of blackmail.

During the negotiations for the Maastricht Treaty in 1989–90, there was a great debate about how to ensure fiscal prudence amongst the participating states as it was clear that electors would be unwilling to bail out automatically any profligate members. Several safeguards were incorporated in the Treaty, as well as adding the Stability and Growth Pact. The current Greek crisis has demonstrated that these safeguards were inadequate and this author argued strongly during the Maastricht Treaty negotiations that it was inevitable that they would be insufficient.

The essence of the debate then was whether fiscal rules operated by a committee of Finance Ministers would ever be used vigorously enough against one of their fellow Ministers – right up to the point where they might be challenged for interfering in a State's internal affairs. The alternative approach was to rely on the discipline effect of the financial markets as they would eventually refuse to lend additional funds. But that approach was dismissed on the grounds that it would only operate late in the day and be highly disruptive in suddenly cutting off funds.

This author wrote several papers in 1989–93 that were published by Salomon Brothers. These argued that the prudential supervision system should be appropriately modified to protect the EU's financial system from becoming overexposed to a failing state to the point that the eurozone could be blackmailed into finding a way to bail out the profligate state. These proposals for a progressive enhancement of market discipline created a stir at the time but were felt to be a step too far as it was far more convenient to believe that no EU state would ever ignore the advice of its fellow members and risk falling into default.

Principles of supervision

The paragraphs below summarise the principles that were developed in some detail 20 years ago, but the details would need to be comprehensively updated to take account of later legislation to deal with the vast expansion, and increased sophistication, of the financial markets. These concepts could be turned into reality quickly because they do not need any amendments to the Treaties. They can be enacted by Parliament and Council, acting upon a proposal from the Commission, as they are simply amendments to existing Directives and Regulations. There are four elements:

1. Recognise the fundamental difference in the nature of the public debt issued by a state that cannot print the money in which it will repay the debt.
2. Structure the prudential regulation of the EU's banking system so that it will be discouraged progressively from financing fiscal excesses by a Member State.
3. Apply corresponding safeguards to other financial institutions that invest the retirement saving of EU citizens in public debt.
4. Develop necessary flanking measures.

The sections below expand these elements and then describe a basic proposal.

Recognise the fundamental difference in the nature of the public debt issued by a state that cannot print the money in which it will repay the debt

This differentiates eurozone members from all other EU and G20 members so international agreements must be enacted into EU legislation in a way that takes account of that fundamental, intrinsic difference. Greece has just proven that there is credit risk in the debt of member states that cannot print their money.

The UK has demonstrated the opposite case – which also applies to all non-eurozone EU, G20 etc states that print their own money. The central bank – even if acting on its own initiative – chose to create £200 billion (around 13% of GDP). It will fall to the historians to dissect the eventual results of this manoeuvre.

The belief that there is no *nominal* credit risk in a state's debt denominated in money that the state can print is embedded in the earliest Solvency Directives of the EU, flowing over from international agreements at the Basel Committee of Banking Supervisors. That was completely correct at the time, but the advent of a monetary union *automatically* invalidated that analysis for the members of the common currency. However, the terms of entry – and subsequent monitoring via the Stability and Growth Pact – were designed in the hope that this theoretical risk never crystallised in practice. Greece has demonstrated that the hope was misplaced.

Structure the prudential regulation of the EU's banking system so that it will be discouraged progressively from financing fiscal excesses by a Member State

The current/imminent (as proposed by BCBS) prudential regulatory approach to banks embodies three elements:

- **Capital adequacy**
  There is still fierce debate on the definition of items that should be counted as capital and the actual quantity.

But there is no debate on the treatment of assets that are obligations of central government and the text from the Capital Requirements Directive (CRD I) is set out below and shows that exposures to central government need have no capital backing – due to the assumption that there is no *nominal* credit risk on loans held to maturity.

Directive 2006/48/EC – ANNEX VI: STANDARDISED APPROACH

Part 1: risk weights: exposures to central governments or central banks

2. Subject to point 3, exposures to central governments and central banks for which a credit assessment by a nominated ECAI is available shall be assigned a risk weight according to Table 1 in accordance with the assignment by the competent authorities of the credit assessments of eligible ECAIs to six steps in a credit quality assessment scale.

Table 1

Credit quality step	1	2	3	4	5	6
Risk weight	0%	20%	50%	100%	100%	150%

3. Exposures to the European Central Bank shall be assigned a 0% risk weight.

- **Liquidity**
  The planned major increase in required holdings of liquid assets can be fulfilled by holding securities issued by sovereigns. The BCBS proposes that the complete requirement for holding liquid assets can be satisfied by holding *"Assets are considered to be high quality liquid assets if they can be easily and immediately converted into cash at little or no loss*

of value." The definition is set out in the box below and again follows the 0% risk weighting concept. However, Greece has demonstrated that such assets may turn out not be so marketable.

BCBS: International framework for liquidity risk measurement, standards and monitoring – consultative document, December 2009

Definition of liquid assets

34. The stock of high quality liquid assets should be comprised of assets which meet the characteristics outlined above. The following list describes the assets which meet these characteristics and can therefore be used as the stock of liquid assets:

(a) cash; (b) central bank reserves, to the extent that they can be drawn down in times of stress; (c) marketable securities representing claims on or claims guaranteed by sovereigns, ... as long as all the following criteria are met:

(i) They are assigned a 0% risk-weight under the Basel II standardised approach;
(ii) Deep repo-markets exist for these securities; and
(iii) The securities are not issued by banks or other financial services entities.

- **Large exposure and concentration rules**
  A standard part of banking regulation (and of other financial institutions) is to limit the proportion of their assets that can be exposed to any single borrower or connected party. Naturally the explosion of financial sophistication has meant that such rules have had to become ever more complex to see-through structures to the underlying assets. Correspondingly, there are rules to prevent an overexposure

of a bank's assets relative to its capital. In general, such rules are waived when the exposure is to the central government.

Apply corresponding safeguards to other financial institutions that invest the retirement savings of EU citizens in public debt

Similar principles about concentration and overexposure to a public debtor should be applied to insurance companies, pension funds and all types of mutual funds where citizens entrust their savings to intermediaries to ensure a diversified pool of assets. However, this should not detract from the liberty of an individual to invest in a fund that is specifically designed (and clearly labelled) to invest in riskier assets such as loans to deteriorating states.

Develop necessary flanking measures

- Auditors would be expected to certify – to regulators and stakeholders – that such regulations were being complied with.
- Irresponsible behaviour by states and their officials should be subject to personal sanction. The same standards of responsible behaviour and knowledge should be expected from Ministers and their officials as from Boards of Directors of say banks and those senior executives that have a 'significant influence' on the conduct of the organisation's affairs. Wrong behaviour in misleading investors is still wrong even if the motive is patriotism, rather than personal greed.

The basic proposal

The forthcoming revision to the Capital Requirements Directive (CRD IV) gives a legislative opportunity to change the treatment of banks holding government exposures when that government becomes subject to the EDP due to its deteriorating finances. The essence of the EDP procedure is set out in the box below and the key is what happens if the State fails to comply with the Council's recommendation – see the emphasised section. Self-evidently, that government's debts have become more risky than they were, so the proposal is that any new debts (or roll-overs) would incur a capital charge *automatically* and corresponding limits be placed on exposures to this new debt.

On each occasion when the state fails to comply with the Council's recommendations, the riskiness must be presumed to have increased so the credit quality would be *automatically* (perhaps subject to an override by a super-QMV) moved down a 'quality step' by the CRD IV rules. Thus any eventual decision to impose sanctions would also be accompanied by a 'junk' capital backing and exposure limit. Moreover, exposures to that state should be marked to market so the rising level of its interest rates would compel banks to increase their provisions against that borrower, diminishing their appetite for further losses.

There would be a presumption that the ECB would match the eligibility rules for its 'repo' facilities to correspond to the official perception of increasing riskiness.

As this process would take a number of years, the relevant government would have time to adjust but would also be fully aware that if it went to the brink of default, then the EU's banking and financial system would have adjusted to that risk already and would not be undermined. Ideally, at the brink of default, the EU financial system would have a relatively small exposure and would be fully provisioned already.

The Excessive Deficit Procedure (EDP)

If a Member State exceeds the deficit ceiling, the EDP is triggered at EU level. This entails several steps – including the possibility of sanctions – to encourage the Member State concerned to take measures to rectify the situation. The EDP is established in the Treaty and specified in the Stability and Growth Pact legislation.

Identifying an excessive deficit…

The EDP sets out criteria, schedules and deadlines for the Council to reach a decision on the existence of an excessive deficit. This decision is taken within a fixed time period after the deadlines – of 1 April and 1 October – for EU Member States to report their government finances to the Commission. No EDP procedure will be launched if the excess of the government deficit over the 3% of GDP threshold is considered temporary and exceptional and the deficit remains close to the threshold.

…and requesting the Member State to correct it

When the Council decides that a deficit is excessive, it makes recommendations to the Member State concerned and establishes deadlines for effective corrective action to be taken. The Council monitors implementation of its recommendations and abrogates the EDP decision when the excessive deficit is corrected. *If the Member State fails to comply, the Council can decide to move to the next step of the EDP, the ultimate possibility being to impose financial sanctions.* [Author's emphasis]

Source: European Commission

Appendix II: The Graham Bishop papers

Fiscal Constraints in EMU – September 1993

The drive to EMU has slowed – not halted – and the Maastricht Treaty mandates the completion of detailed secondary legislation by year-end. Decisions that are about to be taken will influence the structure of the EC's financial markets, irrespective of the existence of EMU.

Valuing Public Debt in the EC: EMU Benefits Versus 'No-Bail-Out' Risks – November 1991

The Treaty should require the regulations governing the EC's financial system to take full account of the new risks in public debt. Investors can then look forward to major benefits from EMU.

The EC's Public Debt Disease: Discipline with Credit Spreads and Cure with Price – May 1991

In a single currency world, a key credit test will be the proportion of a member state's income spent on interest payments. Markets will discipline excesses and require higher interest rates. Price stability – with lower real interest rates – will cause a remarkable leap in credit quality.

1992 and Beyond: The Creation of an EC 'Hard Money' Union – July 1990

EMU will have to be a 'hard money' union dedicated to price stability. For EC member states, successful borrowing will depend on sound financial policies.

1992 and Beyond: Creating and EC Monetary Union with Binding Market Rules – February 1990

A plan to ensure that market discipline is certain, yet operates slowly and progressively. This plan proposes specific measures to strengthen the structure of the financial system sufficiently that a Member State's default is not disastrous.

1992 and Beyond: Market Discipline Can Work in The EC Monetary Union – November 1989

Lessons from other monetary Unions (Canada, Australia, West Germany); the New York City crisis of 1975. The market can be a more effective sanction of fiscal profligacy than binding rules.

www.ingramcontent.com/pod-product-compliance
Ingram Content Group UK Ltd.
Pitfield, Milton Keynes, MK11 3LW, UK
UKHW040227290926
15471UKWH00001B/35

9 781907 720147